MINDFULNESS IN 8 DAYS

MINDFULNESS IN 8 DAYS

How to be Happy and Find Inner Peace
in an Unpredictable World

Second Edition

Kathirasan K

Marshall Cavendish
Editions

© 2023 K. Kathirasan and Marshall Cavendish International (Asia) Pte Ltd

First published in 2017

This second edition published in 2023 by Marshall Cavendish Editions
An imprint of Marshall Cavendish International

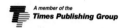
A member of the
Times Publishing Group

Other Marshall Cavendish Offices:
Marshall Cavendish Corporation, 800 Westchester Ave, Suite N-641, Rye Brook, NY 10573, USA • Marshall Cavendish International (Thailand) Co Ltd, 253 Asoke, 16th Floor, Sukhumvit 21 Road, Klongtoey Nua, Wattana, Bangkok 10110, Thailand • Marshall Cavendish (Malaysia) Sdn Bhd, Times Subang, Lot 46, Subang Hi-Tech Industrial Park, Batu Tiga, 40000 Shah Alam, Selangor Darul Ehsan, Malaysia

Marshall Cavendish is a registered trademark of Times Publishing Limited

National Library Board, Singapore Cataloguing in Publication Data
Name(s): Kathirasan, K.
Title: Mindfulness in 8 days : how to be happy and find inner peace in an unpredictable world / Kathirasan K.
Other Title(s): Mindfulness in eight days | How to be happy and find inner peace in an unpredictable world
Description: Second edition. | Singapore : Marshall Cavendish Editions, [2023] | First published: 2017.
Identifier(s): ISBN 978-981-5113-83-9 (paperback)
Subject(s): LCSH: Mindfulness (Psychology) | Stress management. | Meditation. | Well-being. | Human comfort.
Classification: DDC 158.12--dc23

Printed in Singapore

CONTENTS

FOREWORD

Mindfulness is about cultivating awareness of the present moment, so that we can meet ourselves and others with kindness and compassion. Compassion is the key to a happier, more meaningful and peaceful life. Without being present, you can't hope to cultivate this quality.

In this book, Kathirasan guides you on a journey of mindfulness and compassion over eight transformative days. Eight days may seem like a short time, but ultimately you don't even need eight days. You just need this moment.

Right now, and in every waking moment, you have the choice to be consciously aware of the outer world and your inner landscape, or to go back to thinking down those well-worn neural highways of your mind. Thoughts about what you have to do, or what you should have done. How good you are or how bad you are. And all the time, in front of your very eyes, a unique miracle is unfolding.

With well-chosen quotes, wise words of encouragement, and easy-to-do daily activities, this book will awaken your senses, calm your mind and open your heart to a more nourishing and sustainable way of living.

You're in for a treat!

Shamash Alidina
Author of *The Mindful Way Through Stress*
and *Mindfulness for Dummies*

INTRODUCTION

This book is probably one of the shorter manuals you will find on understanding and practising mindfulness. Mindfulness is the awareness that is always available in any given moment. This awareness is enhanced through paying attention to and practising acceptance of the experiences in the present moment, without any judgment. Mindfulness allows us to be self-aware while we go about the affairs of our lives. In short, mindfulness is an awareness practice.

The rewards of mindfulness practices are twofold. Research has shown that mindfulness can greatly reduce stress levels and help regulate negative emotions. Secondly, by cultivating self-awareness, mindfulness practices can enhance our quality of life, and help us be happier.

I was first introduced to mindfulness and meditation in the late 1990s by a Himalayan teacher. It had a tremendous impact on me, transforming my worldview and my perceptions of success and failure, stress and joy. I was at that time a very unhappy person. In trying to cope with life's challenges, I had ended up in a state of constantly wanting more in terms of everything I experienced.

I wanted people to love me, I wanted success and to be recognised for it, I wanted to be rich. I was not able to accept rejections, failures and people who were different from me. Striving for these goals and ruminating about what I did not want left me stressed and eventually unhappy. I was demanding so much from myself and demanding so much from the world and the people around me.

And all that time, I did not know who, or what, I was. Everything I knew of myself was defined through the eyes of others. When people found me useful, resourceful and good, I felt good about myself. My self-perception was defined through the perception of others. In fact, I did not want to know why I was perceived as 'useful, resourceful and good' but their evaluation of me was good enough for me as it gave me the feeling that I was desirable and an acceptable person.

After learning mindfulness, all this changed. I became more self-aware, and with that came the ability to confront difficult situations with poise, and to treat myself and others with more compassion.

Where I once demanded so much of the world, I now discovered joy within. In fact, I started discovering aspects of myself which I never knew existed. This was not something that happened overnight. It happened over time, gradually, and it continues to happen till this day. Every experience gets 'processed' through Awareness, Attention and Acceptance. These three A's allow me to either let an experience be or interpret it differently through the lenses of my purpose and meaning. Through this dispositional ability, I have gained and continue to gain insights every day of my life. I have become a lifelong learner of the Self as opposed to assuming that my happiness is a destination. I continue to see my happiness as a journey centred on *Being* rather than *Becoming*, because happiness is experienced in the present moment.

All of these effects, since the time I started practising mindfulness, positively influenced my career, my emotional health, and the relationships I had with people. I became less demanding and more accepting of oneself, others and the world. I started to realise that compassion, empathy and kindness are three spokes of being, knowing and acting in the world. In no way did mindfulness lower my own standards of the good life, which I believe to be a universal human experience. It shed more light on the interconnectedness of human lives, where I don't see another person as an 'other'. I see everyone as a form of 'being' just like me. I gained a new clarity of purpose and an understanding of the different roles I play in life.

With mindfulness, I also found a renewed appreciation for everything the world has to offer, including the 'undesirable' things. I began to see the desirable and undesirable experiences presented to me by the world as two sides of the same coin, one dependent on the other for its existence. In fact, I learned to see experiences as products of my interpretations, and to recognise that many perspectives were possible, none greater than the others, though I also learned to see value in taking perspectives that conduce wellbeing and happiness. These changes led me to start teaching mindfulness practices, long before they entered mainstream media.

When the COVID-19 pandemic hit, it was a great test of my mindfulness practice, way of being and awareness. On reflection, I am surprised by the way I responded to it. The three years of restrictions, which included total lockdowns, social distancing and being COVID-positive (for two weeks), taught me a great deal about myself. My wife (a mindfulness teacher and practitioner like myself) and I were hardly bored with the lockdowns and travel restrictions. To our surprise, we never felt that any of these changes affected our state of being. We were very comfortable being at home and not stepping out unless necessary, such as to walk the dog, buy groceries or go for medical appointments. We found a stability within that had little to do with what was happening outside of us.

Our household income was reduced and our livelihood was impacted, but we lived within our means with no qualms whatsoever. I started to adapt by using technology to compensate for face-to-face meetings and learned more skills to facilitate and teach mindfulness virtually. I was also able to upskill the mindfulness teachers at our centre. On the whole, the three years of pandemic brought great lessons as I continued to meditate and reflect on my Self with the insights gained.

*　　　*　　　*

Several years before COVID, in 2016, my experiences and experiments with secular mindfulness had led me to develop the eight-week Mindfulness-Based Wellbeing Enhancement (MBWE) programme.

Most of the people who came to my MBWE classes looked weary, dissatisfied, conflicted or lost. By the time they were midway through the MBWE programme, almost everyone said that their life had taken a noticeable positive turn. Some started appreciating their spouse more. Some started to notice behaviours that were contrary to values they held close to their hearts. More than a few told me that they finally knew who they were. And these discoveries led them to recognise the possibility of being happy. And all that I taught them through the MBWE was not to change themselves but to accept the Self as it is, and notice the changes within. By merely accepting, noticing and being aware, change happened for them.

Mindfulness has become one of the most researched contemplative practices of the last three decades. With increasing evidence of its effectiveness, you may be more inclined to try out some mindfulness practices. Hence, I decided to write this book as an offering to the world, to encourage you to experiment with mindfulness in your everyday life and in your own way. Or perhaps you wish to know what mindfulness is before embarking on a full-fledged intensive programme.

I have met people who were sceptical about mindfulness, assuming it to be another New Age fad. I resonate strongly with them, as it is better to approach any practice with scepticism until it is proven to be valuable to you. There is no single solution that can solve all of the world's problems. There is no one path for everyone to take; each of us has to find our own path. I invite you to find your path from the insights you gain from this book.

This book is for you if you seek:

- a glimpse into the world of mindfulness before deepening the exploration,

- a self-paced mindfulness experience, or

- to dip your toes into mindfulness.

This book takes the form of eight experiments with yourself over eight days. It will help you by being an opportunity to enter into the world of mindfulness in the privacy of your own home, your office or even on your daily commute. You can read the book at your own pace – you don't have to do all eight days in a row.

If you happen to be attending an eight-week mindfulness program such as the MBWE, MBSR, MBCT, etc., you can use this book to supplement your weekly reading, perhaps reading one chapter per week. And if you choose to do so, you may skip the invitations to practice found at the end of each chapter as you will be given daily home practices specific to your eight-week mindfulness programme.

The only thing I ask is that you approach these practices with an attitude of open-mindedness and a willingness to experiment. Be like a toddler that ventures to experience everything in its path with genuine curiosity.

I wish you joy on this journey.

DAY 1:
BEING CURIOUS

You are on a flight to your holiday destination. The pilot has welcomed everyone onboard, introduced his co-pilot and crew, and announced the estimated arrival time. You sit back and relax.

Little do you realise, apart from the pilot and co-pilot, there is another pilot in the cockpit with them – a non-human one, the 'autopilot'. This pilot has no heart, and neither does he have a brain like yours. And yet he knows your destination like the back of his hand and needs no control from the human pilots.

The moment the pilots get into the cockpit, the autopilot is just a switch away. All that the pilots need to do is to switch him on, and the autopilot works his magic.

We, too, have an autopilot in the pit of our brain. Our autopilot manifests when we do things in a mechanical manner without awareness.

Do you brush your teeth feeling the bristles of the toothbrush on your gums and teeth? Do you shower feeling the contact of water on your skin and feeling the touch of your hands as you soap yourself? Or do you cruise through these daily activities with your mind on other thoughts?

Your autopilot, although it steers you through these activities safely, prevents you from being fully in the moment. You could be reading the newspapers and upon finishing you realise you finished a whole cup of tea without any recollection of tasting it at all. When you are on autopilot, you deprive yourself of the opportunity to fully experience and enjoy the journey called life.

Worse still, without being aware of it, your thoughts and actions may be hijacked by this autopilot. Sometimes we regret our actions and hold this regret for the rest of our lives. Recall a situation when someone said no to an idea or suggestion of yours. Your mind may have assumed that the no was a sign of rejection in spite of knowing it was actually just a simple no to your idea and not you as a person. This personalisation possibly made you dramatise this incident to yourself and others. I remember catastrophising events in my life, which sent me on a downward spiral.

This is again your autopilot in action. It can prevent you from seeing what is there, replacing it with what is not there. The autopilot has taken over our lives, and we cannot seem to take back possession.

Though I have presented autopilot as something negative, I must acknowledge that the autopilot is not a bad guy all the time. In times of emergency and danger, he does help by making quick decisions to save us, like withdrawing our hand from fire.

But when we have our autopilot in the 'on' position all the time, we lose our attentiveness to our daily affairs, such that we do not remember the journey anymore. All we are interested in is the destination.

'HE WHO KNOWS OTHERS IS WISE;
HE WHO KNOWS HIMSELF
IS ENLIGHTENED'

– LAO TZU

One of the key benefits of mindfulness is that it allows you to reclaim the driver's seat of your experiences and start being 'fully there' in every moment and every experience. The simplest way to do this is not to fight your autopilot but to gently start with practices that focus your attention on the present moment.

We have the ability to pay attention to almost anything in our life. All we need is an intentional mind wanting to pay attention to any experience or activity. The simplest of things can be magnified into something profound just by paying attention to them. Imagine the experience of scientists when they first looked into the microscope to study the pollen in plants. A new world opened up to them just by magnifying attention. As the father of American psychology, William James, said:

'The faculty of voluntarily bringing back a wandering attention, over and over again, is the very root of judgment, character, and will…. But it is easier to define this ideal than to give practical directions for bringing it about.'

His statement astutely acknowledges that while it is important to direct attention flexibly, we may not know how to do it. Indeed, it was for me. I remember my mother taking me to task for being careless in the way I responded to test questions in primary school. She kept repeating, 'You need to pay attention or you are going to fail your exams.' I asked her how I could do that. She told me, 'Just pay attention.' But I went blank as I did not know how to pay attention and what to pay attention to. Every time I forced myself to study or do my schoolwork, my sense of aversion grew.

If only I had learned that cultivating attentional strength is just like how we walk into a gym to work on our muscles before using it in our daily life. It is the sustained and regular workout in the gym that strengthens my muscles and enables me to better manage my health. In the same way, mindfulness training takes place by paying attention to our own bodily sensations, thoughts, urges and emotions, which are our internal gym, open 24 hours a day, 7 days a week. It is through this training that you come to a better understanding of yourself, your relationships with other people in your life, and the world you live in.

Mindfulness helps us to recognise the value of the present moment, which we often miss while going about 'living' our lives. But are we really 'living' our lives at all?

So busy are we moving from one task to another that we forget to value each moment. I could be so wrapped up in answering an office email at home that I ignore my child right next to me yearning for my attention. We are more often mere passersby of our own lives rather than people who are living with the full experience that life is offering every second.

In fact, I have stopped searching for a 'purpose' for living my life since mindfulness dawned on me. Instead, I find that the purpose is 'in the living' rather than in seeking an answer. When I dropped that search, I suddenly started living my life more purposefully and meaningfully. I began to notice what made me happy, unhappy, fulfilled, satisfied, dissatisfied, content, excited, exhausted, etc. Every moment was a potentially life-changing experience. Mindfulness is the beginning of living and the end to searching.

How is it that such a simple thing as paying attention has become so difficult? Have you seen how infants crawl and pick up objects to observe as if they have never seen these objects before? In fact, that's exactly what it is: they have never seen those things before. That innocent, childlike curiosity is what we have lost. The child cries when it is hungry; it doesn't cry because of, say, a lack of food in storage for tomorrow. The child is only interested in the present, exploring and experiencing whatever life presents.

'YESTERDAY'S THE PAST,
TOMORROW'S THE FUTURE, BUT
TODAY IS A GIFT. THAT'S WHY
IT'S CALLED THE PRESENT.'

– BIL KEANE

Imagine how it would be if this childlike curiosity that is grounded in the present moment could be coupled with the maturity of our adult life experiences. This is definitely a recipe for a great mindful life.

And yet, we often neglect the present moment, unconsciously obsessed as we are with the future and the past. We fail to realise that the present moment is what creates the past in the form of memories. The same present moment forms the reference plane for our thinking about the future.

All of our thinking takes place in the present moment. We think about the past and about the future in this present moment. As you are reading or listening to this book, it is happening in this very moment. Indeed, the present moment is one of the very few things in life that we can be very certain about.

The present moment can be free from both anxiety and regrets, as all the regrets and sorrows we carry are centred in the past, while all our anxieties and worries are centred in the future.

The present moment is also without time, because you cannot measure it. Try picking up a stopwatch and measuring how long it takes to be 'present'. The moment the clock starts ticking it has become the past.

We cannot hold on to the present moment either. All we can do is just *be* in the present moment.

HOW TO BE MINDFUL

The first step towards being mindful is to bring these three principles into your life:

- Set the intention to practise mindfulness.

- Practise mindfulness by paying attention and bringing acceptance to the Self and its experiences.

- Cultivate the attitudes that enable the practice.

These are the three core principles of mindfulness. They are the foundations for consistent and rewarding practice, as well as the fruits of practice. Mindfulness is the very means and the end itself. That's the reason why we do not behold a destination as we practise mindfulness. It is about anchoring oneself in the very awareness that is always available in any moment.

Mindfulness is an ongoing process, not a finite goal. So don't approach mindfulness as another item in your checklist to be accomplished. Rather, make it a way of living or being.

MINDFULNESS IS 'THE AWARENESS THAT EMERGES THROUGH PAYING ATTENTION ON PURPOSE, IN THE PRESENT MOMENT, AND NON-JUDGMENTALLY TO THE UNFOLDING OF EXPERIENCE MOMENT BY MOMENT'.

– JON KABAT-ZINN

See mindfulness like the way you breathe. Do you have to make a petition every day for your lungs to breathe or does it just happen? Do you have to consciously breathe heavily when you go for a run or does it happen naturally?

Many things in nature just happen, like the sun rising and setting. Natural phenomena do not have an agenda like us humans. They are not motivated by rewards and successes. Mindfulness is best appreciated when you have no real agenda other than wanting to just *be well* and *be happy.* It is indeed a way of living and being yourself, with yourself.

1. INTENTION

Finding your intention behind the desire to learn and practise mindfulness is an important discovery. Ask yourself the following questions:

- Why do I want to be mindful?

- What benefits do I hope to experience by practising mindfulness?

Your answers will provide direction on your mindfulness journey, like a compass. They also provide greater clarity about your values, vision and goals in life. There are no wrong answers to these questions as there could be many reasons for a single action. Your intention for practising mindfulness could be anything from wanting to be healthy to perhaps just wanting to discover myself. While we set our intentions, we do need to expect that they may change over time. That is perfectly normal, because change is a constant.

2. ATTENTION AND ACCEPTANCE

Paying attention is the pivot on which all mindfulness practices rest. It involves directing the mind to a particular object or experience over a length of time. Remember that we can choose what to pay attention to.

For example, if you had to take a train to visit your disagreeable mother-in-law, it would be normal for you to dread the train ride. But the truth is that your mother-in-law is not on the train with you. She is part of the future, not part of the present moment. So *be* the train ride and not drift to the visit ahead. Pay attention to the fields, the activity on the train, your breathing.

This is an opportunity to be with yourself instead of transporting yourself to the future or somewhere you are yet to be.

Acceptance is one of the most unique hallmarks of mindfulness practices. In every mindfulness practice, we allow all experiences to just *be*, with a sense of accommodation. The cultivation of acceptance allows us to respond to life situations with poise, as opposed to jumping to a reaction. We learn to notice bodily discomfort, distractions, rumination, joy, pleasure, excitement, urges, and all experiences without judgment.

Every mindfulness practice involves the deployment of attention and acceptance. Imagine attention and acceptance as a couple waltzing together on the dance floor of awareness. This book will show you how to practise the skills of paying attention and bringing acceptance in particular ways.

3. ATTITUDE

Your mindfulness journey will be a much smoother and more rewarding one if you approach your practices with a healthy attitude. A healthy attitude will also keep you on a steady path in the long run. It has been said that 'Your attitude determines

'YOUR LIVING IS DETERMINED NOT
SO MUCH BY WHAT LIFE BRINGS TO YOU
AS BY THE ATTITUDE YOU BRING TO
LIFE; NOT SO MUCH BY WHAT HAPPENS
TO YOU AS BY THE WAY YOUR MIND
LOOKS AT WHAT HAPPENS.'

– KHALIL GIBRAN

your altitude'. Or it is like that pinch of salt that makes a dish so tasty.

Here are some healthy attitudes that are worth cultivating:

Acceptance

While acceptance is a mechanism found in mindfulness practices, it can also serve as an attitude. It is perhaps the most helpful attitude to secure the sustained practice of mindfulness.

It is certain that during your mindfulness practices, your mind may wander, or your body may be unable to perform certain movements. The attitude of acceptance will allow you to accept these shortcomings and march on with your practice.

Acceptance also relates to being in the present without comparing your practice with the past or with your ideals of the future. There is no perfect practice that I am aspiring towards.

This also means that you don't compare your practices with the practices of others. You are unique and so is your life a unique one. There is no better reason than this for you not to compare but to accept yourself as you are. This attitude helps us not to reject any experiences and not to form an aversion towards certain experiences. I have also noticed that as much as this attitude promotes the sustained practice of mindfulness, the very sustained practice of mindfulness also cultivates this attitude in a mutual way.

Beginner's mind

Cultivating the attitude of a beginner will allow you to see things anew in every practice. It also prevents you from comparing or benchmarking your current practice with the past. Tell yourself that you are always learning every time you start your practice. The same mindfulness practice becomes a fresh one each time you practise it.

And tell yourself that you are always a work-in-progress. In fact, all of us are. This humility is born of the understanding that there is no real goal to be achieved other than being what we are. A seasoned mindfulness practitioner does not wear a badge of honour. The learner in me will always allow me to be an adventurer instead of a gold miner.

Focusing on what works

We are frequently bent on seeking out things that do not work for us and fixing them. This fault-finding behaviour and the fear of failure can keep us from maturing emotionally. As we practise mindfulness, let us focus more on what is working than what is not.

All of us are individually unique and hence we need the ability to latch onto what works for us. This is not a one-size-fits-all approach. As you practise, you will likely find that some of the practices resonate stronger with you than other practices. And that is okay. It is important that we cultivate a practice that works for us rather than forcing it on ourselves, only to be unable to sustain it in the long run.

Trust

In spite of all the empirical evidence that mindfulness works, you might doubt it in moments when your mind gets distracted, sleepy or bored. In such moments, your trust in the process of mindfulness will keep you going. Read up on the journeys of other mindfulness practitioners and their results

– you can find numerous first-hand accounts in books and on the internet. Their stories will inspire you to trust this way of being.

It is also important to trust your experiences because they are yours. Only you know what you are experiencing during your mindfulness practices. Bringing this experience to corroborate with the evidence we have for mindfulness can be helpful. Speaking with a trained mindfulness teacher could also be helpful.

Curiosity

Paying attention becomes a quest for knowledge when it is filled with curiosity. This curiosity may lead you to discover new insights about your body, thoughts, behaviour, emotions and environment — all of which you might never have noticed before. Curiosity is like a mirror that gets cleaned of its dust and tarnish with every practice, reflecting your being more and more clearly. After every practice, you walk out a new person as your self-perception expands and becomes positive with curiosity.

Letting go

Letting go is the opposite of being in control. It has been said that the mountains are as though in meditation, and so are the waters and earth. They support whatever animate and inanimate things they bear not by controlling but by just 'being'. Similarly, there is no effort required in the practice of mindfulness. What's needed is to let go of the idea that you are in control. Our need for control stems from our innate need for security. We like to control people, systems and the environment around us to manipulate our thoughts to feel secure. It is normal to feel this way though it may creep into our mindfulness practices as well.

However, we can keep that insecurity away from our mindfulness practices by letting go of what we experience during our practices by just letting them be. We can be a witness to an experience instead of getting involved in its content.

Non-Striving

Striving is the attitude of excessively and strenuously trying to achieve a state that you are not already in. Non-striving is the opposite, where we do not try to change anything. The awareness that arises through mindfulness practices is a capacity that is always available for you in every moment. The purpose of mindfulness practices is to facilitate the discovery of awareness.

Non-striving also helps us to distinguish *being* from *becoming*. If you assume that only by becoming more aware, more accepting and more attentive are you going to be mindful, then you are certainly going to be striving. This assumption reinforces the belief that we are not where we should be. In fact, you are exactly where you are meant to be. Mindfulness is not something to strive for because it is the discovery of awareness and not the creation of it.

Patience

Many of you would be familiar with the phrase, 'Time waits for no one'. Our race against time never ends, right from the moment we are born. Mindfulness is not something that you should race for or struggle for. Or it may end up being just another rat race. Mindfulness is your very being, and it is always available to one who is available to it. Hence, the intention behind your mindfulness practice could be realised tomorrow, next month or even after a lifetime of practice. Patience also does not mean that we wait forever. The act of waiting also implies that we are constantly expecting some change to happen. Patience is more like watering a sapling every day and letting it grow into a tree at its own time. The key to sustained practice is patience.

Kindness

While kindness is always assumed to be of more value when it is shown to others, it is equally important that you are kind to yourself. More often than not, we bring appraisals of our behaviour, thoughts and feelings into our mindfulness practices. There are no standards of right behaviour, right thoughts or right feelings when practising mindfulness. With kindness, we accept all our bodily sensations, urges, thoughts and emotions. I personally find that once we are kind to ourselves, we begin very naturally to be kind to others.

Gratitude

Be grateful for being you and for having the opportunity to practise mindfulness. Be grateful to the people in your life for enabling you to have your private time with yourself while practising mindfulness. Bring gratitude to even the smallest of acts that people do for you. Our existence depends on so many beings, sentient and insentient, in this world. We are not islands. We live in an interconnected world where the social relationships we have contribute to our wellbeing.

For example, I am grateful to the stranger at the mall who took the effort to smile at me before I did. I am grateful to my wife for helping me choose an appropriate shirt for a business meeting. I am grateful to the birds outside my window for making sweet music in the mornings. I am grateful to the cabbie who ensured that I arrived safely at my destination. The list goes on and on...

Non-Judgment

Non-judgment is an attitude we bring to the experience of paying attention every time we practise mindfulness. We do not evaluate the quality of our practice at any point during our practice. There is no good or bad practice; all there is is just practice. Any kind of evaluation over the practice is suspended. For example, we do not manipulate our breathing so that we can improve it. It is common practice in psychotherapy to encourage taking deep breaths when someone feels overwhelmed, but in mindfulness or mindfulness-oriented psychotherapy, attention is directed towards focusing on the breath without changing the breath in any way.

In fact, by just noticing the breath, the breathing rate slows down by itself. There is nothing that needs to be done except to pay attention to each in-breath and out-breath that happens naturally. The same attitude applies to noticing bodily sensations. We notice whatever sensations that are found in the body at this present moment. We do not judge these sensations as bad or good. In the same manner, we also do not judge our thoughts as they rise and fall in our practice as either good or bad. We allow them to be as they are as we continue to notice them moment to moment.

PRACTICE 1

NOTICING WITH CURIOSITY

This practice can be done anytime, anywhere.

1. Start noticing the environment you are in.

2. Bring curiosity into the exploration.

3. You may notice people or things or perhaps the palm of your hand.

4. See them as if you have never seen them before.

5. Start noticing the tiny details that you normally do not notice.

6. Perform this practice for about three minutes.

Post-practice inquiry

1. What were your thoughts during the practice?

2. Was it easy to be curious?

3. Did you make any involuntary judgments about the people and things that you noticed?

DAY 2: HOLISTIC WELLBEING

We all wake up in the morning hoping that the day ahead is going to be a good one. This instinctive desire is shared by all living beings. Like plants seek out light even when placed in the shade, we naturally seek out happiness and wellbeing.

What is wellbeing, and is it different from happiness? Happiness is the personal experience of being satisfied or having satisfied a desire. It denotes a psychological experience. Wellbeing on the other hand refers to something that is universally good for people and ethically informed. While happiness is possible even when doing something wrong like robbing a bank and gloating about that accomplishment, wellbeing does no allow such a possibility, as doing something that harms others would not be deemed to be wholesome.

However, both happiness and wellbeing are important elements in our lives. The former informs us that we are experiencing a *psychological state* in the present moment while the latter provides a *structure* for being happy. This is what I mean by holistic wellbeing.

Our wellbeing and happiness are important to us; sometimes we only realise that we are not fulfilled when we experience unhappiness and prolonged negative emotions. With mindfulness we can bring awareness to our present levels of wellbeing. It can constantly inform us of the aspects of our lives that we are satisfied with and the aspects that we are not. The purpose of mindfulness is not to get you into a mode of *doing*, to remove the causes of unhappiness or to secure the objects of happiness or desire. Rather, mindfulness helps us to be *aware* of the current state instead of reacting to it unawares.

A simple example of this phenomenon could be being bored at home. One of the reactions to boredom is to find something to do, which could be anything like browsing social media, finding someone to meet, watching a movie, listening to music, etc. Instead of reactively *doing* these, mindfulness allows you to dwell on the boredom by noticing how it manifests in your body as sensations, the corresponding urges, the emotions and the thoughts that ensue. This same awareness can be brought to a happy experience as well.

This awareness leads to the generation of insights about what your disposition is. Knowing your disposition helps you to live your life aligned with your purpose and meaning. All of us value different things, and through the things we value and seek, we come to know whether our disposition is hedonic or eudaimonic. A hedonic disposition could mean that I value and seek the pleasures in life, enjoyed through engagement of the sensory organs. A eudaimonic disposition could mean that I seek to realise the virtues of life as my prime pursuit. Each of us would have one of these two dispositions dominating our intentions and actions. The disposition is innate and does not deserve any judgment whatsoever. Bringing awareness to your own disposition allows you to acknowledge who and what you are essentially.

This is exactly what mindfulness does: bring awareness to your disposition. By knowing this, we learn not to adopt someone else's disposition and not to make others adopt our disposition. Instead, we accept that two people, even if they are of the same family or a couple, can be different.

NON-JUDGMENTAL VISION

It is in our nature to give value to things that may not have intrinsic value. This is how we start hobbies like collecting stamps, figurines, or cards. The stamps by themselves are just tiny slips of paper with designs printed on them, but through our likes and dislikes we create value in them. We value some more than others.

This is exactly the reason why we choose to give great respect and adulation to the CEO of a company but don't do the same for the office janitor. While the roles of the CEO and the janitor may be different, the individuals taking on the roles are fundamentally the same. Both of them wake up in the morning and wish for a great day ahead. Both of them desire happiness in their lives and form relationships – just like everyone else.

But the CEO appears to be of greater value than the janitor. How can we see beyond people's roles and view them non-judgmentally? In my years in the corporate world and community work, I have encountered people from all walks of life, from the leaders of countries to people who have not been as fortunate as the average man in terms of their quality of life. I have worked with prison inmates, the elderly in assisted-living homes, the financially challenged and the emotionally weary.

In my heart of hearts, my perception of all of them has been as human beings pure and simple, with the sole difference being what they have and not who they are. Today, someone might be a prisoner, but tomorrow or in the future perhaps he could be a successful entrepreneur.

People may change, but their innate being does not change. When interacting with people doing their jobs, I tell myself that I am relating to their functional roles. At the same time, I take care to maintain the non-judgmental vision that we are all fundamentally the same.

MISCONCEPTIONS OF MINDFULNESS

There are numerous misconceptions about mindfulness and all of them tend to mislead people into assuming that mindfulness is something other than what it is. Here are some common misconceptions:

1. MINDFULNESS IS MEDITATION

Often people conflate mindfulness and meditation. They are similar and different. Meditation refers to a category of contemplative practices. Staring at a light source, concentrating on an object in front of you, listening attentively to music with eyes closed, repeating a set of syllables or name mentally, etc., would all qualify as meditation. Mindfulness, on the other hand, is a specific type of meditation that is distinct from the aforementioned practices. Therefore, mindfulness is a type of meditation, but not all types of meditation are mindfulness. Whenever you encounter the word 'meditation' without qualifications in this book, it refers to mindfulness.

2. MINDFULNESS IS FOR RELAXATION

Often mindfulness is touted to be for relaxation, but technically that is not its primary purpose. Relaxation is a secondary outcome of mindfulness, like the way you feel contented after being out on a dinner date. The primary purpose of the date was to spend quality time with your partner, though the dinner was incidental and therefore secondary. In the same way, the primary purpose of mindfulness is to enable a new relationship with thoughts and your whole self, though relaxation is commonly experienced after every practice. As I often tell people, 'You don't need mindfulness to relax. If you wanted to relax, you can go for a massage, spa, watch a movie, or listen to music.'

3. MINDFULNESS IS EMPTYING YOUR MIND

Mindfulness is not for the purpose of emptying or stilling the mind. Mindfulness builds a new relationship with thoughts and self. This can only happen with thoughts and not without them. Mindfulness practices do not make you avoid, reject or alleviate thoughts.

4. MEDITATION USING EXTERNAL AIDS

Unlike many types of meditation that may use external aids such as music, aromas, flames, a person, etc., mindfulness does not heavily rely on such aids. Instead, in mindfulness practices we use our internal resources that are always available as the objects of meditation, i.e. thoughts, emotions, sensation and urges.

5. MINDFULNESS IS A MAGIC PILL

I have encountered people and organisations who assume that mindfulness is a magic pill or a silver bullet for all their ills. It is important to see that mindfulness supports people in solving a fundamental and perhaps very important problem, which is the way we relate to thoughts and the self. It does not solve all problems. Just like how physical exercise is very important to our wellbeing but it is not going to repair broken relationships or workplace productivity challenges. There is no single solution for all of life's problems, but there are specific solutions for specific problems. Mindfulness is one such solution that works on the self through the self.

6. MINDFULNESS EFFECTS CANNOT BE MEASURED

Contrary to popular belief, the effects of mindfulness *can* be measured. The most popular method is self-reported assessments. Participants take an assessment before a mindfulness programme and then complete another assessment after the programme. The researchers then study the self-reports to find out if there are any significant changes.

With the advancement of technology, today we can also measure the effects of mindfulness through functional magnetic resonance imaging (fMRI) scans. Neuroscientists have been studying mindfulness practitioners by studying the visible changes in the brain scans.

NEGATIVITY BIAS

There is a part of our brain which dominates our emotional reactions and our actions. It is called the amygdala. Neuroscientists consider the amygdala to be the least developed part of the brain in terms of its evolution and behaviour. In fact, one neuroscientist referred to it as the 'reptilian' brain, in the sense that it has not evolved beyond the way reptiles behave, and continues to trigger in us the 'survival' response to fight, freeze or flee. These are our instinctual behaviours related to aggression, dominance, reaction and territoriality. These are traits we share with animals.

The amygdala dominates most of our behaviour when we are faced with challenging situations. If there is one word that best describes its effect, it has to be 'reactive'. It causes us to be reactive and impulsive.

The social psychologist Jonathan Haidt likens the behaviour of the amygdala to an elephant and our executive abilities to its rider. The reactive tendencies in our brain are very much stronger than our executive abilities. That is how powerful the amygdala is. We usually do not display these reactive instincts in our daily interactions. But when danger or threat looms, the amygdala kicks in, and we immediately flee, freeze or fight. This happens so quickly and instinctively that we do not notice it.

In the years that I worked with prison inmates, one recurring theme came up: their remorse over their reactive behaviours which landed them in trouble. It was the untamed brain that got the better of them.

None of us are immune from this problem. However, as human beings, we are endowed with the ability to use the executive abilities of our brain more than the amygdala. This ability resides in the prefrontal cortex, the part of our brain that controls 'response', as opposed to 'reaction'.

ARE WE HUMAN BEINGS OR 'HUMAN DOINGS'?

In the scientific name for our species, *Homo sapiens*, the word 'sapiens' means 'wise' in Latin. This is supposedly our crowning glory. With our innate capacity to be wise, we created great civilisations. We continually develop new technologies and systems that make our lives better. Our high degree of self-awareness has contributed to our survival, evolution and dominance of the planet.

But are we really so wise? We wage deadly wars against each

other, we build societies that oppress the weak, we enact laws that curb our innate nature, we toil away at jobs that make us sick with stress and anxiety... At times I wonder if we really deserve to be called *Homo sapiens* at all.

'WE ARE WORSE THAN ANIMALS,
WE HUNGER FOR THE KILL.'

– LEMMY KILMISTER

It also seems ironic that although we are known as 'human beings', we are always in a state of *doing* rather than *being*. It appears to me that we are programmed to always do one thing or another.

Our lives predominantly revolve around either creating or acquiring new things, destroying old or unwanted things, and modifying things to be the way we like. We also spend quite a bit of time moving from place to place exploring the wonders of new experiences. And after we have rested enough, we look for new things to do. This doing mode is unconscious and relentless. We have a long 'To do' list. How about a 'To be' list for a change? Try making one like this:

TO ~~DO~~ BE LIST

List of things	How will I try to be?
1. Brushing my teeth	I will experience the sensation of the bristles rubbing against my teeth and gums.
2.	
3.	
4.	

Mindfulness provides us an opportunity to be true to the name of our species by restoring the 'beingness' to our human state. As you would have noticed from the exercise above, being is never separate from doing. The opportunity to be is always available while you are performing an action. We should not go away thinking that doing is a bad thing. Doing is important as it creates change in our lives, especially positive change. The problem is *doing without being*. As we practise mindfulness, we learn to see and align our doing with being. We then see doing arising from our being as opposed to it being inspired by a mindless state.

In the practice of mindfulness, we recognise the state of awareness as neither doing nor non-doing. It provides a great opportunity to *be* rather than to *do*, and to discover what we are.

INTRODUCING THE BODY SCAN

The body scan is one of the core mindfulness practices. It is one of the simplest and yet most rewarding of all mindfulness practices, in my opinion. The body scan is practised by bringing attention to different parts of the body. This practice is valuable for several reasons:

BODY AWARENESS

Our daily routines have radically disconnected our mind from our body. We often choose to ignore the sensations of the body as we busy ourselves with our routines. Think of the hurting back, the stiff neck and the tightening chest that you have been ignoring for the longest time.

The body scan allows us to reconnect with our body and its sensations, to 'listen' to our body without judging it. The body has a life of its own. All you can do is put food in your stomach, and the rest of it is taken care of by your body. You do not have to give an order, 'Digest now'. The body scan allows us to appreciate this body that has served (and is serving) us so well. Without it, we would not have been able to come to know and experience the world we live in.

FROM 'DOING' TO 'BEING' MODE

When practising the body scan, think of your body not as an instrument of action but as an instrument for experience. By practising it lying down on the floor, you let go of all the control instincts that you typically exert over the body. This is a good opportunity to honour your body without exploiting it for any other purpose other than simply letting it be.

ATTENTION TRAINING

The training you receive while in the body scan is in acceptance and attention, both of which are very useful in life. Without external objects to focus on, the mind learns to fix its attention on a particular part of the body by being aware of the sensations, as well as to shift that attention to various parts of the body at will.

EMOTIONAL RELEASE

Mental stress has been found to cause physiological symptoms such as tense muscles, body aches, insomnia, chest pains, and many more. One of the ways out of this predicament is to bring awareness to the various parts of the body and in so doing free both the body and mind of its afflictions.

EMOTIONAL METER

By doing the body scan, you will become sensitive to the relationship between stress, emotional pain and the way it manifests in your body. When you monitor these sensations as if on a meter, noticing their rise and fall, you may be able to identify issues that are lodged unconsciously in your mind. This is an avenue for great insights into your private universe.

BEING COMFORTABLE IN YOUR SKIN

With your eyes closed and your mind focused, you will not have time to judge yourself. Over a lifetime, the body goes through three stages: growth, maturity and ageing. Can we learn to accommodate each of these stages gracefully? Can we be comfortable in our own skin? Yes, we can, by gradually embedding the practice of body scan into our lives.

PRACTICE 2

SHORT BODY SCAN

All you need for this practice (and for all other mindfulness practices) is yourself. Initially you may want to use an audio track to guide you through the process (you can use the audio guide from www.centreformindfulness.sg). Then, when it feels right for you, you may like to do this practice independently.

The body scan is practised by bringing attention and acceptance to different parts of your body in turn. You start by bringing your attention to your right big toe and then to the other toes. Then you slowly shift your awareness to the sole of your foot, ankles, shin, calf muscles and so on all the way to the top of your head.

Ensure you are in an environment where you have the least external distraction.

1. Lie down on an exercise mat or a flat surface comfortably with your eyes closed.

2. Start your practice by mentally noticing the different parts of your body.

3. Prepare a sequence based on the sections of your body, for example:

    - left leg
    - right leg
    - back of the torso
    - front of the torso
    - left arm
    - right arm
    - neck
    - face
    - back of the head

4. Start by noticing each of these parts of your body and the sensations there for a minute or 30 seconds before moving on to the next section. (In order not to watch the time during your practice, wait till you've completed the entire body scan before you look at how much time you took altogether and adjust your pace in your next practice.)

Post-practice Inquiry

1. Were you able to notice the different parts of your body?

2. Did your mind get distracted?

3. How did you bring acceptance to the sensations you noticed?

4. Was it easy to do this practice on your own or would it have been easier with a step-by-step audio guide?

DAY 3:
RESPONSABILITY

'ResponsAbility' is the *ability* to *respond* with discretion to the various situations in our lives, instead of reacting to them in a purely 'reptilian' way. Every time you get triggered, you could take a mindful pause and see if you can respond in that situation. This may be useful when reprimanding your child for a misdemeanour or perhaps before taking your colleague or staff to task for a job not well done.

With mindfulness it becomes easier to take this pause, though it may be elusive currently. As we continue to practise mindfulness, we can take this pause in every situation. It will gradually become second nature. Consistent mindfulness practices help to create this gap between stimulus and reaction. You do not have to look for it anymore. It just happens in every experience.

'BETWEEN STIMULUS AND
RESPONSE THERE IS A SPACE.
IN THAT SPACE IS OUR POWER TO
CHOOSE OUR RESPONSE. IN OUR
RESPONSE LIES OUR GROWTH
AND OUR FREEDOM.'

- VIKTOR FRANKL

With *responsability* you will be able to make better decisions in your own life, in the effort to correct your child or improve your staff's performance, instead of lashing out at them in anger and producing not only no improvement in their behaviour and regret on your part, but also a lasting habit of rash outbursts.

Brain scans have found that regular mindfulness practices change the brain structure: the amygdala becomes under-active, the prefrontal cortex lights up with activity. This is another great reason for practising mindfulness. The transformation happens in the brain, thus creating new neuro-pathways for behaviour.

With consistent mindfulness practice, you will be able to make wise decisions without being carried away by your reactive instincts. *Responsability* will help you be in control of any situation instead of being controlled by it.

SELF-INQUIRY

Inquiry in mindfulness is the process of asking questions so as to see things as they are – clearly, objectively, without judgment. Seeing things as they are is all about deepening our curiosity to know and appreciate things in the present moment. If a glass of water is right in front of us, we learn to see this object as it is right now, not how it will be in the future or how it was in the past.

Though we often inquire about and into things in the external world, about facts and figures, seldom do we inquire within to know ourselves. When we inquire within, we pose questions to ourselves. These questions allow us to penetrate into the deeper recesses of our minds, and help us understand our own behaviours, emotions and thoughts.

I had a participant in one of my mindfulness workshops, Sophie, who was going through a tough time. Among other things, she shared that she did not like to be at home in the evenings. I invited her to inquire into this behaviour, without any judgment, for the sake of understanding herself better. I encouraged her to write down her observations in a journal.

The next week when she turned up for the class, Sophie was all smiles. She told me that she had found out something about herself.

The first thing she inquired into was the reason why she did not like being at home. Her answer was that she did not find happiness at home. Or rather, she could not be happy while being at home. It was this unhappiness that drove her to be away from home as much as possible. Let us note here that it was an emotion that caused that specific behaviour.

'THE SCIENTIST IS NOT A PERSON WHO GIVES THE RIGHT ANSWERS, HE'S ONE WHO ASKS THE RIGHT QUESTIONS.'

– CLAUDE LEVI-STRAUSS

And what caused that unhappiness? She shared that this feeling had started when her aged mother moved into her home. Since then, she had not had the privacy to be with her husband as she liked it to be.

She added that her mother was insensitive to her needs, and never gave her the space she needed. She found out that what she valued was her personal space, to not be inhibited by others. She also valued the time she could be with her husband.

These were Sophie's thoughts. Despite this unhappiness, she looked happy sharing her findings from her inquiry with me. She told me that when she asked those questions of herself, she found an awareness about her feelings and beliefs that she never had before.

In fact, she realised that this issue with her mother was the baggage that she had been carrying all her life. Her marriage and her mom's eventual move into her home facilitated this discovery.

With this new clarity, she saw that she did not need to shake these issues off her back. Instead, the discovery of her deeper values was enough to lift Sophie out of her gloom. She shared this reflection with her husband and felt even better that he understood her better now.

Self-awareness is power. The awareness of your behaviours, emotions and thoughts is practically Self-knowledge. It has the power to induce positive changes in you effortlessly and naturally – without you having to strive for change. And it all starts with self-inquiry.

We need to be careful, however, that our inquiry is not for the purpose of finding a victim to blame or for judging ourselves. Though this might be how a court session or police interrogation is conducted, it is not the purpose of self-inquiry.

Inquiry is about being genuinely curious. Children naturally display this curiosity when they ask endless questions. As we become adults, we hesitate to ask questions for fear that we may appear ignorant or be judged.

Asking questions can be truly revelatory for the questioner. For a single question, there can be many answers. Each of them will reveal new perspectives. That's the reason counsellors, psychotherapists and coaches ask so many questions instead of telling us what to do. By asking ourselves questions, we counsel ourselves. Remember Sophie? Be your own trusted friend.

THOUGHTS ARE THOUGHTS

In the mindfulness practices so far, have you encountered difficulty maintaining your attention? Did your mind wander? It is natural for thoughts to naturally creep into your head when you start concentrating your mind in mindfulness practices. I remember getting frustrated in my first few practices.

In my mindfulness workshops, people often share with me that they are unable to meditate because too many thoughts intrude on them during the practice. I tell them that that is precisely the reason why they should be meditating.

The mind that does not wander does not need meditation. It is the average person like you and me who needs meditation. The nature of the mind is to wander. Do you expect to stand in the middle of a highway and not see any traffic? The mind is a thought highway. Sometimes you see a truck, sometimes a motorbike or a luxury car. They come in different sizes, shapes and colours. But they are all vehicles nonetheless, regardless of their differences. Thoughts are like these vehicles. Some big, some small, some significant, some trivial and the list goes on. All of these vehicles have the licence to be on the road. It is the road where they belong. Would you buy a vehicle and keep it in storage?

Similarly, treat your thoughts in your mindfulness practices with equanimity because they are exactly where they should be. See those thoughts as simply thoughts. They may enter your mind with different messages, suggestions and even memories of the past. Treat them all the same. They are only thoughts after all – they come, and they go.

The more importance we give to a thought, the heavier it gets. The heavier it gets, the more it weighs on us, and the more stress and anxiety is induced. The more we try to reject it, the more it wants to linger in our mind space. It is like a dog that gives chase when you run away from it. But if you treat the provoked dog mindfully, you'll get away scar-free.

So, welcome all thoughts into your mind during your practices. Do not fight them to leave. Do not force them to stay either. Let them leave when they want.

CULTIVATING EQUANIMITY

When something goes wrong, and we feel upset, we are actually bothered not so much by our action itself as by the outcome of that action. It is the spilled coffee, the failed examinations or the failed relationship that bring negative emotions to our minds. Similarly, it is the successes, achievements and accomplishments that bring us positive emotions, as they are outcomes of actions.

Being equanimous is about keeping the mind open to all types of outcomes, and accepting all outcomes regardless of the judgments we make of them. Why do this? Firstly let's acknowledge that all our actions may produce four types of outcomes in relation to our expectations. For example, I might go to a shopping mall wanting to buy a pair of jeans that I've always wanted.

- The first possible outcome is that the jeans are available for sale at a price that I can afford.

- The second possible outcome is that the jeans are being sold at half of my budget.

- The third possible outcome is that the jeans are being sold at twice my budget and hence way beyond what I can afford.

- The fourth possible outcome is that the jeans are sold out.

In summary, we experience four types of outcomes:

- As expected

- Better than expected

- Less than expected

- Opposite to the expected

Now ask yourself, how might you have responded in each of these four situations? More often than not, when the outcomes are less than expected, our mind goes into a negative spiral of emotions. We get upset, disappointed, sad or frustrated over such outcomes. Worse, these emotions often have a spillover effect on other aspects of our lives. They affect those around us, including our loved ones, and can even ruin our entire day. All because our expectations were not met.

But the problem is not with our expectations. As much as we often hear people asking us if our expectations were high or low, we can't stop having expectations. In fact, expectations are a type of desire, and they operate as a wish or want. Both expectations and desire are things that we cannot stop.

On the other hand, it is impossible to perform any action without expecting a result or an outcome. We would not even lift a finger without having an expectation. Desire and expectations are human and hence they should not be seen as a bane.

In fact, the capacity to desire is what drives our civilisations to progress and flourish, to surmount the greatest challenges, and to achieve all our technological advancements. I often say that not wanting to desire is another desire.

The real problem here is not with expectations nor desire but us being unable to accept outcomes gracefully without mental agitation. And this happens especially with the outcomes that are less than expected and opposite to what was expected. We are always fine with the 'as expected' and the 'better than expected' outcomes.

Being equanimous is being able to accept any of the four outcomes without being mentally agitated, without being swayed by our emotions. At times, it is our reaction to the outcomes that makes us act in ways that are less than desirable.

The role of mindfulness is to cultivate this attitude by enabling the psychological mechanism of acceptance toward the four outcomes with equanimity. It is not that you stop being unhappy or happy when acceptance becomes an attitude. Rather, you will not be strangled by these states of mind. You start being aware of these emotions without the need to suppress your emotions. It is like saying 'My mind is disturbed' instead of 'I am disturbed'.

One exercise that helps us be equanimous is to reflect on the insight that every outcome is brought about through the interaction and contribution of multiple factors. Let's say I accidentally dropped a glass of water on the floor, and the glass shattered to pieces. What are the various factors that caused the glass to shatter?

Here is a list of possible factors:

- The glass had to be hard enough for it to have such an impact on hitting the floor.

- The law of gravity had to be present or else the glass would not have fallen.

- The floor had to be a hard surface for the glass to shatter.

- The height from which the glass dropped.

- Myself for initiating the event.

Although there were some five factors that contributed to the breaking of the glass, somehow I chose to zoom in on a single factor, myself, as the sole cause of the accident. This sense of ownership that we have towards all our actions compounds the way we feel towards the four types of outcomes. This happens precisely because we assume that we are the sole cause of a particular effect.

We must bear in mind that this is not an exercise in divesting responsibility for our actions. Rather it is a mental reflection that reduces the load of the sense of misplaced ownership for any given action or its outcomes. I have no control over the laws of gravity and perhaps limited control over that act of negligence when the glass slipped from my hand. Hence the load of ownership is now distributed over many factors including myself.

If you were to extend this thinking to all of your life's experiences, you will realise that almost all of them are contributed to and caused by innumerable factors. You are not the absolute cause of every outcome in your life. Therefore, it is only wise that we do not obsess to find a cause (or someone to blame) for unfavourable outcomes and instead cultivate acceptance, which then leads us to be *Responsable*.

As a result of this, you will gradually cultivate both an acceptance towards all your actions and the ability to see things as they are. This creates the space for you to choose an action as a response instead of a reaction. As you face different outcomes from day to day, you will start being a witness to the states of your mind, and not a prisoner of your judgments.

LIVING IS A MEDITATION

Since you started reading this book, your life may have become a little more meditative or reflective. I call this way of living, 'living in meditation'. It is not that your lifestyle has now become somewhat like that of a monk or a nun. That is not the goal of mindfulness. Nor is it living a life of isolation or solitude.

Mindfulness is about integrating a meditative disposition with your way of life. I know of people who wake up as early as

4 a.m. in the morning to meditate for 45 minutes before starting the day and retire to bed by 8 p.m. Then there are people who wake up at 9 a.m. and go to bed at midnight after a meditation sitting. There is no one-size-fits-all method to make meditation part of your life. Instead of sacrificing your lifestyle at the altar of mindfulness, integrate them both into a harmonious whole, where you do not see living as separate from meditation and meditation as separate from living. Living in meditation is the spontaneous ability to live life mindfully.

Mindfulness does not require a religious subscription. Although it has its roots in the soils of ancient India among the practitioners of Buddhism and Yoga, it has been a secular practice for more than three decades just like how yoga has become secular in the last 70 years.

Yoga has been stripped of its spiritual roots and is now practised widely as a form of calisthenics. Today the benefits of both mindfulness and yoga are enjoyed by people of all faiths. They have become valuable tools in the areas of education, psychotherapy and even professional development.

I have delivered mindfulness programmes to students and teachers, enhancing their performance at school. I have also

'THE EARTH MEDITATES AS IT WERE.
THE SKY MEDITATES AS IT WERE.
WATER MEDITATES AS IT WERE.
THE MOUNTAINS MEDITATE
AS IT WERE.'

– UPANISHAD

guided business leaders in embedding mindfulness into their leadership style. More of these contemplative practices are making their way into the mainstream, and I do expect even more to come in the future.

And the reason for its increasing popularity is that mindfulness allows self-discovery by using oneself as the instrument. While other approaches rely on external aids and people to enable self-discovery, mindfulness uses 'me, myself and I' as the instrument to practise and inquire into. The only apparatus you need is your mind. As long as you have one, you are able to practise mindfulness and be aware.

INTRODUCING
COPING BREATHING SPACE

Coping Breathing Space is a practice especially valuable when your thoughts are starting to move in a negative direction. It can help you when you are in situations such as:

- A tense meeting at the office

- Before an important job interview

- A heated conversation

- Before giving a speech

- Before a competition

- During a tense business negotiation meeting

- A stressful situation

- A sorrowful or shocking event

Just step out of the situation that is making you feel uncomfortable and practise coping breathing space. It will bring your mind back to a restorative state and to the present moment very quickly. All you need is just three minutes.

Coping breathing space need not be practised only when the emotional storm is raging. Instead, it should also be practised when your weather is fine, and the skies are clear, so as to prepare you to cope with the real storm.

PRACTICE 3

COPING BREATHING SPACE

Coping breathing space is best practised in a relatively quiet place.

1. Awareness

- Adopt a comfortable standing posture which keeps your body relaxed.

- Become aware of your body and the surface upon which you are standing.

- Then ask yourself:

  - What is my experience right now in my thoughts? Acknowledge thoughts as mental events.
  - What am I feeling?
  - What are some bodily sensations?

- Acknowledge and accept your experience.

2. Breathing

- Gently direct full attention to your breathing.

- Notice the belly rising and falling with every in-breath and out-breath.

3. Conscious expansion

- Expand the field of your awareness around your breathing.

- Include the sense of the body as a whole, your posture, and facial expression.

Post-practice inquiry

1. Did you feel calm and collected after the practice?

2. How did you keep track of the three minutes?

Whenever you feel stressed, sad, anxious, depressed, or if some other negative emotion is dominating your thoughts, do this practice.

DAY 4: FOCUSING ON WHAT WORKS

Stephen bought a bouquet of his wife's favourite roses to surprise her. They arranged to meet at 5 p.m. at the shopping mall, but the bus Stephen was on got delayed on the way there. His wife became anxious at the crowded mall and when Stephen turned up 15 minutes late, she spat words of disappointment and accusation at him. The conversation between them escalated into a battle of words and in the end, the bouquet of roses never changed hands.

One of the great traits that human beings possess is the ability to look at our failures and improve upon them. This trait in us has advanced all human civilisations and continues to enhance our quality of life through technological advancements and innovations. In our individual lives, too, we often zoom in on aspects that we feel are in need of improvement, correction, eradication.

However, such an approach to advancement does not tap into our greatest potential. These deficit-focused approaches make us feel miserable about who we are. Any efforts at improvement are then motivated by the need to not feel miserable, inadequate or insecure. It is seeking to remove these feelings that prompts action.

'LOOK WELL INTO THYSELF;
THERE IS A SOURCE OF STRENGTH
WHICH WILL ALWAYS SPRING UP IF
THOU WILT ALWAYS LOOK.'

– MARCUS AURELIUS

If you have undergone a performance appraisal at work before, you will know what I mean. Do you remember the feeling when your boss went through the long list of things that you did not do well and how he kept harping on it? I am sure it was not a great feeling to be hearing about 'what you are not good at'.

Now imagine if your boss spent a larger part of the time with you talking about the things you did well and how that contributed to the success of the department. How would you have felt? Would you have felt more motivated to improve and excel? Would your mood and emotions be more positive?

This is an asset-based approach as opposed to the earlier deficit-based one. Research at the University of North Carolina at Chapel Hill has shown that people feel more motivated when the conversations around them revolve around what is working for them rather than what is not.

The challenge, however, is that our brains have a natural negative bias that is entrenched in finding fault and focusing on what is not going well. Like in the story of Stephen and his wife, the delay caused by the bus became the focal point of their conversation. If only they focused on the bouquet of roses instead, the whole situation could have turned out so different.

It takes time and effort to celebrate what is working well in our lives.

With sustained practice of mindfulness, our minds learn to focus on what is right with us rather than what is wrong. The whole world may judge you based on the many roles that you play in your life, and how you may or may not be up to the mark. But how about changing that narrative for a second and looking at what you have done well? There are countless things you have done well. There could also be many strengths in you waiting to be unearthed in the right circumstances.

'THERE IS MORE RIGHT WITH YOU THAN WRONG WITH YOU.'

– JON KABAT- ZINN

The difference between seeing the glass half-empty and half-full is the attitude of the viewer and the flexibility with which you shift your attention. This is exactly what was discovered with long-term meditators. Research tells us that long-term meditators are able to direct their attention to the positive even in times and states where their lives are negative. With mindfulness, you can learn the skill to direct your attention to where you want it, flexibly.

Focusing on what is wrong with us preoccupies our minds with what is not fine, and misery follows. By looking at what works in our lives instead, we can further use that to make our lives better. Here are some tips on how to flip your perspective:

Deficit-based Mindset	Asset-based Mindset
I have lost so much money.	From the lesson learnt, how can I utilise my finances and further grow it or explore other alternatives?
I am not effective at leadership.	Can I learn from specific incidents where I have led people to achieve their goals successfully?

Deficit-based Mindset	Asset-based Mindset
I am not a good spouse.	I must have done well or we would not have come this far. I must recollect the great points of our marriage. And possibly keep doing what I am good at.
I am a good-for-nothing.	What are the areas of my life that I felt excited and energised about? Can that help me in uncovering situations which can help me succeed?

Mindfulness allows us to focus on our assets and remind ourselves that we are unique. Because you are unique, there is no other person like you, and there is a place for everyone in this universe. The ability to shift from a deficit-based mindset to an asset-based one becomes effortless with sustained mindfulness practice.

MEDITATION IS NOT NON-THINKING

There is this widespread notion that meditation is non-thinking. This could be due to the prevalence of modern yoga, which has touted the highest state of meditation to be a state of no thoughts or a suspended state of mind.

I am quite puzzled as to how a state of non-thinking or a suspended state could bring value to our functional life, especially for people like you and me, who very much use our minds to transact in the world and relate with people.

Perhaps a state of no thoughts could give you a temporary respite from all your problems, but wouldn't the state of deep sleep be as good as non-thinking then?

I have always been very wary of people teaching that the aim of meditation is to attain a mystical or superconscious state. While these accounts from practitioners make you more curious about their experiences, they unfortunately reinforce our sense of striving for a change in a future time, as opposed to being in the present moment. We tell ourselves that this supposed state will grant us a psychological freedom that is not available here, right now in this present moment.

Such an approach also reinforces our all-too-common state of being 'human doings' rather than human beings.

Having a far-fetched goal in meditation is no different from any other goal that we set ourselves. Both require you to put great effort into trying to achieve that goal. Such practices have the capacity to create more stress and tension than what they promise to deliver eventually.

It is like treading a path of thorns to reach peace. Spending years walking on such a path can easily be replaced with a path of calm in the present moment.

To give you some context around how these practices of stilling the mind, making it devoid of thoughts through excessive effort, came about, we need to look into the history of meditation. In ancient times, meditation was primarily the practice of religious mendicants and world-renouncing ascetics/monks/nuns/priests. Their lifestyles required them to shun thoughts about the material world and enjoyments. It was for this purpose (as well as others) that meditation was originally taught.

This is certainly not for the common man whose life involves people, enjoyments and materials.

This is the difference between meditation as conventionally understood and mindfulness meditation.

In mindfulness meditation, we have no goal or destination. All that we are focused on is paying attention and practising acceptance in the present moment, noticing our breath, sensations, thoughts and urges. Non-thinking meditation can sound virtuous, especially when it is achieved through much effort. As much as it may be a legitimate goal for the aforementioned people who have a clear purpose for it, it is not so in the case of the common man.

Mindfulness is not being bereft of thoughts and also not expecting the mind to be full of thoughts. Both of these wear us down. Mindfulness helps us to be simply aware and be anchored in the present. I am not searching for any special experience in my meditations or from life. I am just simply 'living in meditation', being aware and responding with my wisdom.

I do not aim to suppress any thought or control it, as this would imply the belief that thoughts are not welcome and unwhole-some. In such a meditation, you end up measuring against time and judging yourself as to how successful you are at struggling to keep the mind thought-less.

Having such expectations is like expecting the highway to be free of vehicles. The highway is meant for vehicles, and in fact especially for uninterrupted high-speed journeys. So it is for the mind. The mind is meant for thoughts. It is not meant to be thought-free.

In fact, I have not found anything this easy in my life. Because I am available all the time to myself, I can bring this awareness anywhere and anytime. As long as I am available, mindfulness is an opportunity.

THIS IS NOT A PRACTICE

I am cautious about using the word 'practice' without present-ing what it means when it comes to mindfulness practices. The word gives the impression that mindfulness practices require you to forcefully make efforts against your will or nature. It seems to suggest that you need to 'drill' yourself, regularly and purposefully.

This could be a big turn-off for some, the idea that mindfulness as a practice is something to be 'done'. On the contrary, mindfulness practices are all about 'being'. Consider how you prepare for bed every night by arranging your pillows, setting the right room temperature and changing into your sleepwear. All of these only set the stage for your sleep. They facilitate your falling asleep, but they do not make you sleep. They create the right conditions for sleep to happen. While asleep you are not consciously aware of the pillows, room temperature or your clothes. You are just sleeping.

Similarly, mindfulness practices are about creating the conducive conditions such that mindfulness happens. As you would have already seen, awareness is always here right now in this present moment – even as you are reading (or listening to) this book. Mindfulness harnesses and realises this potential that we have with us all our lives, like the way curtains are drawn to reveal a stage performance. The curtain does not create or cause the performance. This is a significant feature of mindfulness that many do not appreciate.

Initially, it may appear as if I am setting up an agenda for mindfulness practice, but soon enough you will slip into a mode of spontaneity where practising mindfulness and being aware all the time become effortless.

The practice of mindfulness is also about setting intention, attitude and attention (see Day 1). Do it at a level that feels right for you, without the feeling of being compelled, forced or unhappy.

Hence, we use 'practice' for want of a better word. Once we get out of this practice mode orientation, we start to see mindfulness as a way of being. Gradually we start to appreciate that each mindfulness practice is a date with oneself.

Mindfulness practice is about creating the conducive conditions such that mindfulness happens. As much as mindfulness is usually taught in a group setting for good reasons, I find more comfort and ease in doing my mindfulness practices alone.

Doing them with another person may pressure the other person to conform to my availability in the day, or vice versa. Some practitioners of mindfulness have a habit of comparing how they felt during a particular practice. I have also heard of people comparing how long they were in the seat of meditation and deriving a sense of fulfilment and satisfaction if they have sat longer in a practice than the other person.

Although this may arguably help in tracking our progress, we end up making mindfulness another item on our long checklist of tasks – with clearly defined key performance indicators! Do not judge yourself if you have felt this way or if you have done this before, because that is how we have been taught to measure every activity. All the indicators used at work and in life to measure our 'successes' revolve around how much money we have made, how much savings we have accumulated, how much output we have produced, how much time we have shaved off from the time taken to complete a certain activity, and so forth.

We have made this such a habit that we apply the same 'criteria' to our mindfulness practice. But remember that mindfulness is not something to be 'done', much less a test or a race. So, try to stay away from comparing your practice with others. Instead, you and your fellow practitioners can collectively celebrate the fact that you practised. That fact that you practised is more important than how long you practised. And most importantly, practise every day, even if it is just for five minutes.

INTRODUCING MINDFUL EATING

Mindful eating is a great practice that uses an essential daily activity to bring mindfulness into our lives. I remember once walking into an eatery looking for my favourite food. Having found it and holding the dish on my tray, I walked over to a table to enjoy it.

The next thing I knew, I had finished all the food and could not remember its taste. My mind had been wandering all over, thinking about my tasks for the day and my activities for the evening. Even checking my emails on my smartphone (very smart indeed) between mouthfuls.

On other occasions, I have mindlessly eaten so much food while watching a movie. This was a habit for me.

Mindful eating is all about bringing the mind back to eating with full awareness. I like the way the dishes are served one after the other at Chinese ten-course dinners. It is a great opportunity to bring mindful awareness to enjoying one dish at a time.

Food on the table is a privilege. Let us eat with mindfulness, gratitude and respect.

PRACTICE 4

MINDFUL EATING

You can do this practice with any of your daily meals or even when just having a snack.

First, choose a conducive environment to eat in – one that does not allow you to start a conversation, so that you can bring your full awareness to the meal. Silence is the key, not quietness. You can be silent even in a noisy environment.

Place your personal devices away from sight. Turn off the TV or anything that may distract your eyes or hearing. When you are about to take your first mouthful, look at the food as if you were looking at it for the first time. Notice the ingredients, the colours, the composition on your plate. Enjoy the aromas.

Then place the food on your tongue and chew slowly. Really take your time here. Chew for at least 30 seconds before swallowing. As you chew, pay attention to the flavours of the food. Pay attention to textures as well. Savour the details and nuances of the various components of the dish. Imagine you're trying to extract all the essence from the food.

Engage your hearing too, by listening to the crackle and crunch as you bite into certain foods, and as you chew.

Try this at least once a day, or perhaps with the first three mouthfuls of a meal for a start.

Post-practice inquiry

1. Was this different from how you normally eat your food?

2. Did the food taste different when you ate it mindfully? If yes, what made the difference?

3. What did you learn from eating the food mindfully?

DAY 5: MEANINGFUL ENGAGEMENT

Mindfulness research has revealed a strong correlation between mindfulness and meaning in life. This lines up well with other studies that point out that one's happiness is directly connected to the alignment of one's goals with one's meaning in life. One of the results of mindfulness practice is the discovery of what gives us meaning and being aware of it constantly.

Meaning in life can be defined as simply finding your authentic self – the self that you truly are. Being authentic and engaging in activities that align with your authentic self brings happiness and fulfilment. We may find meaning in raising our children, tending to our family, success in our jobs, or in our spirituality.

I know a lady who finds meaning in serving the needs of her family. To her, feeding her family a good meal means everything. I could clearly see the smile on her face as she went about her chores and the satisfaction in her eyes when someone complimented her cooking.

'IF YOU'VE FOUND MEANING IN YOUR LIFE, YOU DON'T WANT TO GO BACK. YOU WANT TO GO FORWARD. YOU WANT TO SEE MORE, DO MORE. YOU CAN'T WAIT UNTIL YOU'RE SIXTY-FIVE.'

– MORRIE SCHWARTZ

But that does not float my boat. I find meaning in something else. That doesn't mean my meaning is superior or inferior to hers. We each find our own paths to realise meaning in life. Believing that someone else's definition of happiness will bring you joy is a misconception. I've seen couples where one partner exhausts themselves trying to fulfil the other's expectations of happiness. Frequently, people assume that making their partners happy is the key to their own happiness. However, this can lead to misery if catering to your partner's desires isn't your own life's purpose.

It is therefore important that we know what gives us meaning, or we may be on a wild goose chase, forever seeking something or other, not realising that the search itself is the cause of our misery.

At the same time, the discovery of meaning is not something that happens immediately. It is the fruit of awareness, particularly awareness of our motives, intentions, strengths, emotions and values. All these give us an idea of what makes our life meaningful. And as you will have realised from the earlier chapters (and the chapters to come), mindfulness practices over time do just that! They enhance our self-awareness.

Through self-awareness, a sense of clarity about yourself will start to occur. You can liken this to being in a long, dark tunnel, seeing a pin dot of light at the end. As you walk slowly towards it, the dot of light gets bigger and bigger, and finally you are out of the tunnel basking in the sun. Finding meaning is just like this. A growing clarity will take place as you keep practising mindfulness.

Importantly, we need to recognise that the rate of progress may vary from person to person.

I remember a few years ago when it dawned on me that there was a huge disconnect between my strengths/values and my job. It occurred to me that what I really wanted to do was to facilitate the discovery of meaning, value and success for people. And that set me on a transition phase for two years before I formally quit my job to become an entrepreneur and mindfulness teacher.

It is interesting that this happened many years into my practice of mindfulness. But for some of my friends, this happened early on in their journey.

'THE SEARCH FOR MEANING ROBS
OUR LIFE OF MEANING, SENDING US
BACK INTO OUR DISCURSIVE MINDS
WHILE, RIGHT IN FRONT OF US,
THE LAUNDRY PILES UP.'

– KAREN MAEZEN MILLER

The thing is not to compare how fast you find your meaning relative to others. We need to remember always that comparisons inevitably bring self-judgment. As much as finding meaning in life is important to us, we should not treat it as an 'urgent' task.

I like this quote from Dwight D. Eisenhower, who was president of the United States in the 1950s: 'What is important is seldom urgent and what is urgent is seldom important.' There is a lot of truth is his words. Finding meaning is not an urgent task, in the sense of being an item on your checklist to be done as soon as possible.

That's because the search for meaning can in fact rob us of its meaning. Searching takes you away from being in the present moment. For the same reason, we do not search for some unique experience or sensation in our mindfulness practices. We learn to live as we meditate. This is no urgent agenda. All we do is to be in the present moment, living it without judgments. And in time we may discover our meaning.

THE WHOLENESS THAT YOU ALREADY ARE

Before I discovered mindfulness, one of the problems I experienced was a feeling of inadequacy, incompleteness and fragmentation in my life. A feeling that I was not 'whole'. This sense of something lacking in me made me very uncomfortable and frustrated with myself and my life. It made me seek out different experiences, in the hope that the sum total of these experiences would make me whole.

For example, buying a home made me happy at first. And then I thought that by renovating and designing the interiors of my home, I would be happy. After accomplishing that, I told myself that making my home a 'smart home' would make me happy. Having done that, I realised that there was yet another to-do for my happiness. Every time I achieved a milestone, I created a new milestone for myself. I realised that my happiness was short-lived. For example, the sum total of the three happiness 'goals' did not make me three times happier. These external accomplishments did not 'fix' my fragmented self.

In fact, the more I worked harder to satisfy my different identities, it further fragmented my identities, as each of them had their own dreams, goals and desires. The son in me was competing with the brother in me. The employee within was competing with the volunteer role I played. All these separate identities gave me a sense of inadequacy as I realised that they are impossible to be satiated.

Am I a combination of a hundred identities or is there a wholeness that encompasses and holds these parts? The answer to this question was discovered gradually through the insights I gained via my mindfulness practices. As I kept up with the practices, I started seeing that all the so-called parts or roles were connected in and through my awareness, like pearls strung on a thread.

In fact, this wholeness of awareness is what gives all the roles their meaning. As Jon Kabat-Zinn says, 'We are also what was present before the scarring – our original wholeness, what was born whole. And we can reconnect with that intrinsic wholeness at any time, because its very nature is that it is always present. It is who we truly are.'

To know that I am whole – not just a person with various parts, or a person missing some parts – has been very grounding and meaningful to me. You learn to be *aware* of your body, your thoughts, your senses and not *identify* with the body, thoughts and senses. In the same way, you are aware of things that are outside you – the chair, the temperature, the people, the environment. All of them are in your awareness. This awareness is choiceless, as in you cannot *choose* to be aware but just be aware all the time regardless what is presented in its field. The way light functions could be a good illustration for awareness. Light does not create the objects nor choose what to illumine. Any object in the field of light gets illumined naturally and choicelessly.

In this choiceless awareness, you are just plain being, without any identity. In this awareness, thoughts, ideas and perception of your body rise and fall. In fact, your identity of name, position and accomplishments are witnessed in this awareness. Without awareness, all of these are not possible to be experienced.

There are moments in your life when you lose consciousness of your body, such as when you are in deep sleep. In these states, you are just awareness and being, without any conscious ideas or thoughts to perceive. It is not that there is no awareness in deep sleep, it is just that your mind is not there to acknowledge it. This is akin to how your eyes do not report the presence of objects in darkness: it is not that you are not 'seeing' in darkness; you are indeed *seeing* no objects for there is no light.

I see this awareness to be whole because in it I experience all of my experiences. Without it, I would not be able to experience anything, for that matter. It is whole because awareness is homogeneous, and it appears to be fragmented when it identifies with the objects of perception.

I am not referring or alluding to conceptions of a soul or spirituality as presented by various faiths. The recognition of awareness is in spite of your beliefs, not at the expense of it.

While awareness is choiceless, *seeing yourself* as awareness is not an evident fact; it is a choice. Do you see yourself as wholeness and awareness, or do you see yourself as only made up of identities? The former allows you to be part of a greater wholeness and helps you deal with life's challenges very differently from the way you would by possibly seeing yourself as a fragmented self. If you were to see yourself to be like a chariot made up of many parts, then the ground on which the chariot stands is awareness. Regardless of whether the chariot remains as it is or is dismantled, it still depends on the ground for it to be. In the same way, regardless of whether you are happy, contented, miserable or depressed, the ground of awareness is always available to you.

Experiments with mindfulness programmes by people suffering from serious illnesses have produced interesting results. As early as the 1980s, terminally and chronically ill patients at the Stress Reduction Clinic at the University of Massachusetts Medical Centre were led through eight weeks of mindfulness training. These experiments were led by Jon Kabat-Zinn.

At the end of the eight weeks, the patients were able to appreciate their relationships better and were living their lives with renewed meaning. They had found that they could anchor themselves in a wholeness of being beyond their physical ailments. For instance, Kabat-Zinn reported that a cancer patient in the programme meditated that she was not the cancer and an insight dawned on her that she was whole, in spite of the cancer, like the way a broken glass does not lose its intrinsic nature of being glass. Such is the power of the vision of wholeness.

All the mindfulness practices, especially the formal practices such as the body scan, mindful movement and the sitting meditation (a shorter version of sitting meditation, called the awareness of breath, will be practised in Day 6), paves way to the discovery of your intrinsic wholeness or awareness. You will learn to *witness* anything in your mental space when you start recognising this intrinsic awareness.

Therein you will discover the accepting and accommodating nature of awareness, like the way the sky does not reject the clouds regardless of the type or colour of the clouds.

WITNESSING CONSCIOUSNESS

A man was taken to court for embezzling money from his employer. An eyewitness was called in to report what she saw. The judge asked if she was involved in the criminal act. She replied that she had witnessed what happened but was not involved in it in any way.

There is a difference between being involved and being a witness. The witness just reports what happened while those involved in the event are engaged through a sense of ownership and doership. The experience of the witness is being a dispassionate observer of what is unfolding in front of them, like the way the sky witnesses the clouds passing in its presence.

In our lives, we can bring this attitude of a witness to all our experiences before we choose to act or own an event. And this attitude is born of increasing levels of self-awareness gained through sustained mindfulness practices.

In fact, all that we do in mindfulness practices is to witness and notice all our sensations, emotions, thoughts and urges. With a witnessing attitude, pain, pleasure, heat and cold can

'THE CONTACTS OF THE SENSES
WITH THE SENSE OBJECTS GIVE RISE TO
THE FEELINGS OF HEAT AND COLD,
AND PAIN AND PLEASURE. THEY ARE
TRANSITORY AND IMPERMANENT.
THEREFORE, LEARN TO
WITNESS THEM.'

– BHAGAVAD GITA

be reduced to being plain experiences of the sensory organs. You witness them happening without identifying with them. This is similar to the many roles that you have taken up without identifying yourself with any of them.

With gradual consistency in mindfulness practices, the intensity of pain, stress and other debilitating experiences can be greatly reduced by virtue of how we interpret the experience. This has been shown in many modern research experiments.

Furthermore, by adopting a witnessing attitude, one can objectify such experiences without them getting transferred to one's being and trapping us in emotions and thoughts. Saying 'I am in pain' is very different from saying 'The body is in pain'. In the second perspective, you start witnessing the pain by detaching yourself from it mentally while experiencing it physically.

Your being beholds these experiences, but it is not these experiences. I like using the analogy of a projector and its projection to illustrate this. A projection on a white screen depicts many images of different colours and content, but the screen does not change its nature along with the projected images. All it does is to provide a support or background for the projected images. Without the screen, the projection is not possible.

Your awareness is like a projection screen, all blank and ready to receive any sensory experience and to do so without being altered. It just witnesses these experiences, knowing that they belong to the body and senses.

As an athlete during my teens, I sustained a knee injury that prevented me from participating in strenuous activities. The injury soon transformed into a larger fear. I would hesitate to take part in any physical sport at all.

While the pain was physical, the fear it created was mental. A little later in life, as part of my mindfulness practice, I started noticing the pain in my knee. Gradually, the fear of the pain and its possible consequences faded. All that I did was to observe the pain and slowly my mind learned to accept it as part of my wholeness.

Today I jog twice a week and practise postural yoga, setting reasonable limits to my practice. The pain has not completely gone away, but I have learned to live with it. It is no longer a physical or psychological obstacle to my pursuits. As part of the continued way of being a witness, I also started to notice symptoms of muscle atrophy in my lower limbs. As I am slowly crossing half a century of existence, I started noticing pain and weakness in my body. This allowed me to take appropriate action. One of which, interestingly, is to walk barefooted as much as possible. I realised that during mindful walking (you will read about this practice at the end of this chapter), I hardly felt any pain or discomfort. This led me to research a little more about walking barefooted (of course while wearing 'bare-foot' shoes when stepping out of my home) and I found that increasing the frequency of walking barefooted strengthens the lower limbs too. All of this happened to me simply by being an observer. In fact, I realised that by just being a witness, we learn more about ourselves and the surroundings we are in.

A few years ago, I spoke at a school leaders conference. At the end of the session, a few leaders walked away with my business card desiring to stay in touch. A week later, I got a call on my cell phone and on the other end was a school principal who attended that conference. He shared with me a very inter-esting experience, where he had walked into the school on the morning after the session and noticed something about the building that could have posed a safety hazard. He was sur-prised that this hazard had been staring at him for the longest time, but it was only after a few days of mindfulness practice that he noticed the problem.

This witnessing ability greatly reduces the impact that any adverse experience has on us. We stop identifying ourselves with our experiences. Instead, we adopt an outlook of acceptance and accommodation. The second value of this natural witnessing consciousness is the ability to 'know' about ourselves and the things around us. We start noticing things, and that increases our knowledge.

INTRODUCING MINDFUL WALKING

Walking is one of the simplest activities we do. We often do it in a mechanical manner, on autopilot, our minds distracted by thoughts. We hardly observe the way we walk.

In the practice of mindful walking (also called walking meditation), you become aware of walking again. You start paying attention to the sheer fact of balancing your body – something you'll have taken for granted since you took your first baby steps.

You notice the sensations of the contact between the soles of your feet and the ground. You also notice how the contact brings sensations throughout the other parts of your body. While the purpose of walking is to take you from point A to point B, in mindful walking you have no agenda except to walk mindfully and experience every step that you take.

In the words of Jon Kabat-Zinn, mindful walking is 'walking and knowing that you are walking'.

PRACTICE 5

MINDFUL WALKING

I would suggest that you practise this for the first time in the privacy of your home.

1. Stand up straight, barefooted, without straining any part of your body.

2. Feel your feet touching the ground.

3. Distribute the weight of your body on both feet evenly.

4. Have your gaze on the floor without straining your neck.

5. Step out with your left foot. Feel it move, feel the heel touching the ground, now the ball of your foot, now the toes.

6. Feel the same as the right foot comes forward.

7. Walk at a steady pace, slightly slower than your usual. When your attention wanders, bring it back to the sensation of your feet touching the ground.

8. Do this for about three minutes.

Post-practice inquiry

1. How was this different from how you normally walk?

2. Was it easy to stay balanced while walking mindfully? Were you able to notice the sensations on each foot as you rolled it forward?

3. How could you make this an occasional practice in your life?

DAY 6: GENERATING PERSPECTIVES

Ali approached his teacher and sat next to him. The teacher took out a mirror, put it right in front of Ali's face, and asked, 'Who is this?' Ali, with a curious expression, said, 'That's me.' The teacher then pointed the mirror at Ali's chest and asked, 'Who is this?' And Ali said, 'That's me.' The teacher then kept moving the mirror to show other parts of Ali's body. Each time, he asked Ali the same question, and Ali responded with the same answer. Finally, the teacher asked, 'Which one of you is the real Ali if there are so many Alis?'

This brings us to the point about the difference between reality and perspectives. We know that Ali is one, but we can understand and see Ali from different perspectives. In the same way, we can look at situations, experiences and events from different perspectives. Often we get attached to one reality, either refusing to see other perspectives or denying the possibility of different perspectives altogether.

When we stop seeing things and experiences in absolutes, we gain new perspectives. This shift takes place as we see that the only constant in our experience is awareness and that all experiences are happening in the field of awareness and thus we are not attached to any one perspective. We then learn to entertain the possibility and exercise the flexibility to shift perspectives purposefully. Let us use the story of Ali to understand this.

If I were to ask you what part of Ali would indicate that Ali is happy, you might possibly direct me to his face, to see if he is smiling or laughing. How about if we wanted to know if Ali has diabetes? Then we might want to do a blood test to check his sugar levels. We would not look at Ali's face to know if he has high blood sugar. Though Ali is one person, we examine different parts of him to understand different things about him.

In the same manner, our minds, through the strength of mindfulness training, can learn to shift perspectives flexibly and purposefully. In a situation where I am perhaps disappointed or angry, I could learn to look at the situation such that it helps me to be well and learn from the experience, instead of ruminating over thoughts that induce anger or disappointment. Mindfulness gives us the ability to shift and generate perspectives, and choose one that helps us to live with purpose and meaning.

PEACE AND STILLNESS

Right after a mindfulness practice, participants usually hope not to disturb the sense of peace that they discovered over the course of the session. You may feel the same way after trying one or two of the mindfulness practices in this book.

In the stillness, you discover the inner peace that is always available but encountered too infrequently. You discover more and more of that peace that can be experienced in being with yourself.

With this inner peace, I've found that my mind reacts differently to situations. The rise of anger, hatred and other unwholesome emotions has reduced drastically over the years. My perspectives of situations and events have also changed.

It is not that this inner peace makes you unable to express your feelings or tranquillised by stillness. Sometimes you do need the courage to stand up to protect yourself or others in imminent danger. This inner peace allows you to respond to situations with poise rather than reactivity. This is very important in the uncertain world we live in today as many things are so unpredictable, like the way the COVID-19 pandemic showed up when we were unprepared for it.

This inner peace also allows you to get along better with yourself and others. You could relate to people positively and your relationships could become stronger and more nourishing. Confrontational, problem-centred discussions that were once very uncomfortable can transform into energising conversations. Conflicts can be resolved swiftly, if not forestalled altogether.

Sometimes I do feel uncomfortable in situations that exude negativity. But I am able to hold my peace and composure in such situations. In situations where my active involvement is needed, I am able to get excited and energetic spontaneously as a result of my conscious will rather than being a victim of uncontrollable forces.

Your friends and family may notice these changes in you over time as they may not take place immediately. Always remember that acceptance comes first, change later. Acceptance is an involuntary psychological disposition that allows you to let an experience be in your awareness without rejecting it. Acceptance does not mean resignation. Changes like these

'IF YOU CANNOT FIND PEACE WITHIN YOURSELF, YOU WILL NEVER FIND IT ANYWHERE ELSE.'

— MARVIN GAYE

may happen to you or may not, but do not set an expectation for predetermined results. Practise for the sake of practising, and when you do see change, accept that too.

YOU ALREADY ARE
WHERE YOU SHOULD BE

It may occur to you as you keep meditating that in being and awareness, there is no past or future but just the present. All that you have is the present moment. Awareness does not depend on memory, and yet it allows us to access our past through memories in the present moment, like the way objects are seen in light. All thoughts about the future also take place in awareness as it just illumines those thoughts without changing them in any way, just like how light does not alter the object it reveals.

By recognising this, you will also appreciate that you are exactly where you are meant to be. And there is no place you can be without yourself (i.e. awareness) in it. If you do see yourself as awareness, being and peaceful, wherever you go, you will never lose sight of that. It is in the present moment that this happens.

I have heard friends say that they are not happy living in this city and want to move to some other place. If you cannot find happiness in one place, I wonder if you can be happy in another as that place too is subject to change, or in the end you might even change. We are not leaving cities for happiness. All that we are doing is putting ourselves in another place, hoping that a new experience will make us happy, until we look for the next one. Our minds are experience hunters.

The reason for making changes cannot be for want of happiness, as that is a product of the mind and not one of space. People move for the reasons of functional necessity, financial opportunities, and conducive environment, amongst others. These are all perfectly justified and should be done if you feel the need to do so. But mistaking it for happiness and wholeness is getting it all wrong, for you have placed that experience in a future time and place.

All feelings of happiness, joy, fulfilment and contentment take place in the present. And the first step towards it is to recognise that you are already where you should be. In the present moment, you can discover that you are the wholeness of being.

DEVICE DETOX

I'm not sure if you have heard, but humankind has been taken hostage around the world by high-tech intelligent devices. These devices have penetrated into our brains to get us dependent on them. Yes, I am talking about smartphones, tablets, laptops, smart-watches, smart-home devices and other such devices. In fact, I recently introduced a robotic vacuum cleaner in my office. It does its job well, at least most of the time.

But reliance can turn into addiction. And our addiction to smart devices is a classic case of how an awesome invention can rob us of our ability to be with ourselves without any distractions.

I see couples at the dinner table engrossed in their smartphones for minutes without uttering a word to each other. I see children plugged into their tablets and smartphones for hours (possibly so as to free their parents to do their own thing). On the bus or train, I see people playing games and watching movies on their mobile devices rather than conversing with others or just 'being'. A research study found that since the COVID-19 pandemic, children staring at screens has risen by 52 percent.

Honestly, I do not see any problem in these devices as they are not inherently bad. I use a smartphone too; in fact I realised just weeks ago that I do not need a large wallet anymore, now that cash is used less, and I may be able to replace it with a smaller one, just enough for my essential credit cards. My smartphone has all the information I need and even acts as a virtual payment facility. It is how we use these devices that makes the difference in how they affect our mental and even physical wellbeing.

Today, gadgets have become something that we are connected to by force of habit. Anything that causes the mind to be habitually drawn to it becomes an addiction, and hence it is unhealthy for us. In one study, it was found that when a person's smartphone is within reach, even if it is off, cognitive capacity declines. It is quite obvious when you don't have to remember people's phone numbers, events and appointments, or a promise you made. When was the last time you picked up a map to find your way to a location? The mental skill of navigation is not needed as much anymore.

But being mindful means the exact opposite. In being mindful, we bring conscious awareness into our thoughts, emotions, feelings and actions. So while devices are very useful or possibly even indispensable, we do not need them all the time. This is the difference we can make in our lifestyle. Even just witnessing, non-judgmentally, these habitual inclinations can help in drastically reducing our dependence on them. Then, we could find opportunities to 'detoxify' ourselves by putting our devices away at specific times and contexts, for example:

- During meals

- When you are in bed and about to sleep

- When you are walking (for safety reasons too)

- When you are with a loved one

Try taking frequent short breaks from devices at your workplace too. Take a walk to the pantry. Look out of your window at nature or something that is not digital.

GRATITUDE

Gratitude is a human trait that we share with domestic animals. We can learn so much from them. Dogs will not bite the hand that feeds them. They openly show gratitude to us for caring for them.

Similarly, we humans have so much to be grateful for. I am grateful for the sun, which provides us with light and heat; the air that I breathe; the public transport system that I use every day.

An acquaintance once told me that we should be grateful to the ice-cream man for providing us with the opportunity to enjoy an ice-cream rather than expecting him to be grateful to us for being his customer. What an insightful perspective that is!

Even if the subway trains break down from time to time, be grateful that you need not travel to work on foot. Or just be grateful that it has served you well for so many years. Be grateful that you have a team at work or colleagues to interact with instead of complaining about their performance.

In all these cases, being grateful is a magic pill that calms down our mental agitation instantaneously. Gratitude is not just about saying thanks and showing appreciation. It is a way of seeing and appreciating the world as it is. Our lives are not always filled with losses, and neither are they always filled with gains. Our lives meander through the banks of losses and gains. We can be grateful for these changes as none of them stay forever.

There is also this tendency to offer gratitude to people and things we consider ours. Often these come up during gratitude reflections, such as 'I am grateful for my husband, my children, my dog, our home, etc.'. People and things who do not belong to this category tend to be considered 'the others'. It is important that we are prosocially grateful, reminding ourselves of the people and things that are not part of our immediate family, relationships (past and present). These supposed 'others' could be the farmers who grew the food on the table, the subway operators who keep the city going, the builders of roads, etc. These 'insignificant' people become significant when we offer prosocial gratitude.

COMPASSION, EMPATHY AND KINDNESS

During one of my workshops, a participant told me, 'If someone has hurt me, I can't wish them well.' I responded to her with a smile. I'm not sure what she picked up from my smile. But one thing is certain: it's not easy to feel compassion for others all the time.

We are also very critical of ourselves. I remember an acquaintance of mine who committed suicide because he felt he was not good enough in the eyes of his girlfriend. I really wished I had spent some time with him the day before. We could all benefit from a little compassion and kindness.

Whether we feel it about others or about ourselves, compassion is one of the most profound feelings that we as human beings have the privilege of experiencing. Compassion is the deep emotional feeling we experience when we witness the suffering or distress of others. Compassion becomes empathy when we put ourselves in the shoes of others when they go through pain or difficulty, and we imagine how they feel.

Where there is compassion or empathy, it is very difficult to judge others or wilfully cause anyone pain. In my school days, I was an avid soccer player. During one of our games, a teammate of mine suffered a bad foul and fell to the ground. I did not get to see the whole episode of him being tackled, and so when I went up to him, I asked, laughing, 'How did you fall?' In response, he said, 'Instead of helping me, you are having a laugh at my pain?' This event left an indelible mark on me. I understood that when someone is in pain, the first thing to do is to soothe it a little. This act is called kindness.

Acts of kindness are the physical demonstration of compassion. Sometimes we feel compassion for someone in misery but fail to transform that into an act of kindness. For the person who is suffering, our silence can be deafening. Kindness is not measured by how much you did, how many dollars you gave, or how many lives you touched. The fact that you did something is good enough.

Acts of kindness can make a huge difference, whether it's giving money to a beggar, or helping an elderly person with a heavy load, or feeding a poor man. Performing acts of kindness always reminds me of what I am: a human being. I am grateful for being able to feel compassion and wanting to be kind.

'THE WORLD SUFFERS A LOT.
NOT BECAUSE OF THE VIOLENCE
OF BAD PEOPLE. BUT BECAUSE
OF THE SILENCE OF THE
GOOD PEOPLE.'

– NAPOLEON BONAPARTE

I have also been at the receiving end of kindness from people known and unknown to me. This knowledge motivates me to continue being kind, if I need a reason at all.

How do we cultivate kindness? It's easy if we know how. But if you don't, then the trick is to 'fake it till you make it' – which is what a wise teacher told me more than two decades ago. All you have to do is just do it. By doing it, i.e. practising kindness, you develop the ability to make it part of you. From it being 'faked' at the beginning, it will eventually become genuine and natural to you. But isn't 'faking it' unnatural? Yes, it is if you are not in touch with your compassionate self. That's the reason why compassion is such a core value in mindfulness. From compassion alone comes kindness. Without compassion, the act of giving kindness becomes mechanical, without a feeling attached to it. That said, the act of giving kindness mechanically is still worthy, as the receiver benefits from it nonetheless.

You can cultivate and grow this compassionate feeling inside you, watering it daily with mindfulness practices. You cannot force compassion to grow. All you can do is nurture it and allow nature to take its course. And when your compassion is tended well, kindness flowers.

While it is mostly easy to have compassion for people we love or even for people we are indifferent to, it is harder to have compassion for those who have caused us harm.

Like the participant who shared his feelings with me during the workshop, it is only natural to feel that way. It is human to feel so. So in the tradition of mindfulness, we introduce a meditation called the 'loving kindness meditation'. This practice helps us cultivate and grow the compassionate self in us. It can also be used to direct feelings of compassion to people whom we often find it difficult to have compassion for.

At the same time that we talk about compassion and giving kindness to others, we do not forget the giver, which is you. It is equally important, or perhaps more important, that we show the same compassion to ourselves.

In my mindfulness sessions, participants often report that they were not able to keep up with the practice or did not stick to the planned schedule. I remind them to have compassion for themselves and to accept themselves with all their supposed shortcomings – which are nothing but judgments they've placed on themselves.

I also remind them not to forget their intention behind their mindfulness practices. Being aware of our intentions and cultivating the attitude of acceptance are two of the important elements of practising mindfulness. I invite you to do the same.

INTRODUCING AWARENESS OF BREATH

Our day begins the moment we get out of bed and start getting things 'done'. The 'human doing' in us does not rest until we go to bed again. It sometimes seems we are in a constant race against time.

Awareness of breath meditation allows you to disengage yourself from 'doing' and engage yourself in the 'being' and 'awareness' that you are. This is a wonderful opportunity to be in touch with the 'being' that has been 'doing' everything all through your life. It is a respite from your active mind and body.

In the practice of awareness of breath, you will experience moments of peace and stillness. Discovering this will allow you to recognise your being as peaceful, tranquil and still, even amidst activity. This is what I earlier called 'living in meditation'.

Meditation is one of the rare practices where the idea of gaining something is not there. You are naked and bare, without desire to accomplish anything other than what you already are. It is a wonderful opportunity for self-awareness and non-striving.

PRACTICE 6

AWARENESS OF BREATH

Awareness of breath is an extension of the breathing space practice introduced on Day 3, and it is also a shorter version of the sitting meditation.

In this practice, we pay attention to our breathing; we are not forcing or manipulating it. Instead, we just let breathing be the way it is, and effortlessly bring our attention to it.

1. Find yourself a comfortable seat.

2. Gently tell yourself that you are now seated, with a clear intention to focus on your breathing for the next five to ten minutes.

3. Start observing your breathing without deliberately changing its rhythm or pace in any way.

4. Just notice it with genuine curiosity. There is no goal in this practice except you being in the present noticing your breath.

5. Perform this practice for about five to ten minutes.

If your attention wanders away from your breath during this practice, bring compassion and kindness to your practice by accepting this tendency of the mind.

Post-practice inquiry

1. Did you like the practice? Why?

2. Was the seat comfortable? Did you have to make adjustments to your seat to be comfortable?

3. Were you kind to yourself every time your thoughts wandered?

DAY 7:
MINDFUL LIVING

Mindful living is all about bringing the attitude and insights gained from mindfulness practices into daily life. It enables us to look at life in a different way and discover things that we have missed all our lives. By leading a mindful life, we live each day as if it is a new one and welcome all its experiences. Here are seven things you can reflect on and gain insights to live mindfully.

PRACTICE

The only way to learn to ride a bicycle is to ride a bicycle. No amount of theoretical explanation can make you master riding a bicycle. It is by trying, making mistakes, falling down, getting hurt and retrying that we master the skill.

Over time, having mastered riding, we are no longer conscious of the riding anymore. We use the bicycle to make journeys to many destinations. We can ride it even on rough terrains.

Mindfulness is rather like learning to ride a bicycle. Having mastered it, we can make our journey of life mindful without any conscious effort. We can learn to navigate through the rough terrains of our lives and to also appreciate the smooth terrains that we take for granted.

And all of these start with practice. Practise mindfulness daily without fail. Even if it is for a minute, do it.

The brain is like a muscle. The more we flex it, the stronger and healthier it gets. This is due to the neuroplasticity of the brain, which scientists discovered about 50 years ago. The moment we stop flexing it, it withers. Our brains contain white and grey matter. Increased volume of white matter is responsible for cognitive decline and dementia. The grey matter is associated with higher processing and further mental development. As we age and step into our senior years, the white matter increases in volume naturally. In recent research, it was found that grey matter increased in volume with two to four weeks of mindfulness practice.

Bring this attitude to all areas of your life – at work, at home, at social events. You can start by:

- Mindfully turning these pages as you read this book

- Mindfully listening to people as they speak

- Enjoying your cup of tea by mindfully sipping it

It is through these baby steps that we gain mastery without having our focus on the eventual goal of mastery.

BEING COMFORTABLE WITH SILENCE

I cannot understate the value of silence. Most of us shun silence because we are not comfortable with it. We often attempt to find something to do whenever we encounter silence.

Try this: Close your eyes now and enjoy the silence for the next three minutes. Did you enjoy the silence? Or did your mind compel you to do something to engage your senses? For most of us, it would be the latter.

Somehow, we reserve silence for monks and hermits and don't consider it something for us. Yet, we are the ones who need it most, living as we do amid the hustle and bustle of urban life.

Our lack of appreciation for silence could be due to our belief that silence is not valuable economically. It is not going to feed you, earn you money or solve your life problems. I beg to differ, though. Silence is more valuable for the prime reason that it allows you to feed yourself, earn money and solve problems more effectively.

Silence is like the eye of the storm which is absolutely calm in spite of the powerful whirlwind of energy around it. Silence is like the rest given to a motor or an engine after a long day of ceaseless activity. We, too, need rest to calm down, so that we can work with greater energy and effectiveness. Sleep is definitely an opportunity for rest, but it does not work on our minds as consciously as silence does. Silence is a conscious choice, unlike sleep.

You can make silence available anywhere. All you need to do is shut the door and sit on your bed or your office chair for just five minutes with your eyes closed. Thoughts will rush in and distract you – do not resist them. Accommodate them like an ocean accommodates all rivers.

It is important to acknowledge, however, that being silent for prolonged periods is not healthy. If human beings were meant to be silent, we would not have mouths to speak in the first place. It would be as preposterous to ask a singing bird to stop singing. Being silent is a conscious practice like the way we go for a jog to improve our cardio fitness. We don't keep jogging all our lives. We do it as a regulated practice and not as a tool for relating with people. As we are social beings, communication is the lifeline of our existence. We are not islands.

TIME WITH YOURSELF

As a teenager, we enjoy the time we spend with friends and generally people we prefer to be with. But as we grow up, it seems to get harder to exercise this freedom to spend our time with people that we like to be with. Instead, we seem to be given fixed roles which come with limited freedom, such as being an employee, a parent, a caregiver for elderly parents, a neighbour, a community leader, amongst many others.

These roles do not give us much room for choice. They each carry a set of obligations that need to be discharged whether we like it or not. For example, the moment you become a community leader, the community expects that you give time and energy to the needs of the community, which may rob you of your personal and family time. Every role comes with its obligatory duties. With each new role, your bag of duties keeps expanding.

While it is commendable that we sacrifice our time and energy for others, do we spend enough time with people we choose to be with – and with ourselves? Do we find time to be with friends, loved ones and ourselves without an agenda?

Time with yourself is very important because it allows you to retreat within as well as to reflect on the past and present and think about the future. In case you are wondering, mindfulness is not future-averse. It is during mindfulness practices that we stay present. Planning for the future is very important but we do it with what is available in the present moment.

Commit to spending time by choice. Go for a walk alone in the park or just sit down with your loved ones or your pets. Find something to do that matters to you for the sake of just doing it. We can discover profundity in the mundane too.

RELATIONSHIPS

As I have mentioned, we are social beings. We are prone to forming relationships with people and things of the world. In the course of our lives, we meet many people, some by choice and others not by choice, like the way we had unconsciously experienced the care (or the lack of care) by our parents and caregivers. All of these choiceless and choiceful experiences shape the way we treat the people we meet in our lives.

How can we treat the people we encounter mindfully? One thing that we can certainly learn to do is to try our best not to judge them. Treat every meeting and connection with others as an opportunity to accept and accommodate them as they are.

Yes, you are actually not that different after all from the people you meet. In the present moment, two human beings are just 'beings' searching for the same experiences revolving around the pursuit of pleasure and the avoidance of pain.

The biggest challenge we face involves those who are near and dear to us, and those whom we have invested our emotions in. I have found that it is easier not to judge my staff than my spouse, children or parents. Our loved ones are so close to us that we become too familiar; we take them for granted and judge them incessantly for not meeting our expectations or standards. In the same way, the people we judge also judge us, based on their expectations and standards. This becomes a vicious cycle of non-acceptance and eventually leads to rejection or even separation.

I am sure you are familiar with stories of quarrels over the toothbrush being placed on the wrong side of the vanity counter or with disagreements over points of view. These arguments arise because of accumulated judgments born of dissatisfaction with the other.

To recover the value we have for relationships, we need to cherish relationships by accommodating them without judgment and also noticing what is working well in the relationship.

CHOOSE YOUR ENVIRONMENT

Our environments – whether natural or manmade – have a direct impact on our lives. For those of us who live in dense urban jungles, try to find opportunities to walk through parks or look out of your office window to witness the birds on the trees, the unripe fruits hanging on the branches and the squirrels. Observe the plants as you water them and the flowers that have bloomed.

Let your eyes fall on all of nature and let it connect with you. When I jog in the park near my home, sometimes I jog over to the stream to look at the fishes and turtles. Sometimes I get to see a family of otters.

Research has shown that people who live amidst nature are happier than those who do not. So it is good to introduce some greenery into your home, not just for decoration but also for you to observe and spend time with.

As we go about our day, walking from point A to point B or waiting for the bus or train, we tend to plug into our music or fiddle with our smartphones, sending text messages, browsing social media or playing games. Take a break from this tendency by choosing to enjoy the journey. Watch the people on the crowded bus or train. Feel the moving train. Listen to the sounds around you.

Notice your thoughts as they rise involuntarily upon noticing things around you. Laugh at the judgments that your mind (not you) makes about the guy who looks cool or the beautiful lady opposite you. Notice how one thought leads to another, and then to another.

If you drive, then there is a high chance that your journey is primarily on a fixed route every day. Maybe you could try a different route once in a while and notice the changes. Or perhaps even start noticing with purpose while driving on the same route daily.

THE PRESENT MOMENT

Spend more time enjoying the gift of the present moment. The quickest way to do this is to bring your attention to your breath. Our minds inevitably react to both thoughts of the past and future. Why not take a break from this routine to be in the present, where there is certitude?

The wonder that you are can only be seen in the present. The universe opens itself in front of you just because you are there to witness it. Witness everything as if it was meant to be witnessed by you.

To bring this attitude into your life, start by noticing your breath. It has been with you since the time you took your first breath, and your lungs have been working ceaseless since then. While our heart, lungs and many other organs have been with us from the womb, functioning to the best of their ability, it is our breath that is easiest to notice, because of its tangible movement. The breath does not seek your permission to be. Breathing just happens, not by our choice.

'THE ULTIMATE VALUE OF LIFE
DEPENDS UPON AWARENESS AND THE
POWER OF CONTEMPLATION RATHER
THAN UPON MERE SURVIVAL.'

– ARISTOTLE

NOTICING YOUR EMOTIONS

Instead of rejecting the unpleasant emotions in your mind, witness them like they were never yours. Like the body, which has a life of its own, the mind too has a life of its own. Like a monkey, our minds can make a circus out of our life experiences. In fact, it is quite unpredictable as to what emotion will arise in a given situation.

While emotions have the power to enter your mind, you hold the power to let them stay or leave. This includes your positive emotions too. You can choose to direct attention to an emotion and empower it with choice when you start noticing it with curiosity.

Emotions are like guests entering your doorway. No guest stays forever. They have to leave someday. If you do not entertain them, they will leave. So just watch those unpleasant thoughts come and go.

Noticing our unpleasant emotions helps us to stay disengaged from those emotions, thus reducing their negative impact. Noticing our pleasant emotions helps us understand what causes them and what our values, purpose and principles are.

PLEASURE AND PAIN

Pleasure and pain – these two experiences dominate our lives. We are driven to seek the one and to avoid the other. We believe that in so doing, we will achieve happiness and be free from suffering, unhappiness and misery.

What we do not realise is that underlying any experience of happiness or unhappiness is a more fundamental phenomenon happening each moment:

Experience = Feeling/Thought/Sensation + Interpretation

Every feeling, thought or sensation is interpreted through our mind. The agreeable and the disagreeable are not inherent in the sensations but a result of our personal evaluations superimposed on them. The same sensation can be interpreted differently depending on our evaluation. Isn't it strange that the pain felt during a body massage is welcome, but a similar chronic pain in your body is not? What we deem to be agreeable or disagreeable is primarily based on how conducive we consider it to be to our wellbeing or to our cherished values and beliefs.

Often, we associate the agreeable with happiness and disagreeable with unhappiness, which is itself an error. This is also connected with assuming the pleasurable to be always good and the painful to be always bad. This can result in avoidant behaviour that has the potential to become compulsive.

THOUGHTS ARE NOT YOU

Liying was elated to win the first prize at her university's Innovation Challenge. As she went up on stage to receive the much-coveted prize, her mother Zifeng, who was sitting in the audience, was overjoyed. After the presentation, Zifeng, still beaming with pride, mingled with the other guests. However, she started to attract many disapproving looks as she boasted loudly to everyone about 'her' achievement. It came to a point that Liying went up to her mother and said, 'Please, Ma, it was I who won the prize, not you.'

We identify ourselves with the successes and failures of our children, partners, spouses, parents and so forth. We feel bad when they feel bad and good when they feel good. It is a good feeling when some of the gold dust of people we know intimately rubs off on us. It is as if their successes and achievements have become our own. That is probably the reason why people love hanging out with the rich and famous.

This identification happens internally too. We choose to identify with specific thoughts that mean a lot to us. For some, the thought of being fat will become an identity issue; for others, it could be being poor or rich, stupid or intelligent.

It is not that the thought of being fat, ugly or stupid is a problem. It is identifying with that quality that is the problem. When you say, 'I am fat', you have made the quality of fatness a defining part of you. And this limits you to a narrow definition of yourself. It limits and confines your thoughts, your beliefs about your abilities, your relationships with others, and your potential to be a whole human being. You are more than the fatness that you have identified with. You are so much more than that – more than any number of labels can define.

Some of us also identify ourselves with the thoughts of others. A single statement made by someone can ruin our day. We feel that our entire self is being judged. In reality, no statement has the power to ruin our day until and unless we have empowered it by identifying with it. So what if someone called you 'incompetent'? It remains a thought until you choose to identify with it.

Thoughts are just thoughts. If we can recognise that, we should also see that thoughts are not us. To identify yourself as your thoughts – or the thoughts of others – is a mistaken identity. Thoughts are what you have, not what you are.

'A JOY, A DEPRESSION,
A MEANNESS, SOME
MOMENTARY AWARENESS
COMES AS AN UNEXPECTED
VISITOR. WELCOME AND
ENTERTAIN THEM ALL!'

– RUMI

Mindfulness practices help us to disassociate ourselves from our thoughts. We learn to objectify them and stop seeing them as part of our identity. This disassociation is not to divest ourselves of responsibility for actions that ensue as a result of our thoughts or emotions. Rather the disassociation is to create a healthy distance from your thoughts.

Remind yourself: Thoughts arise in me, but I am not the thoughts. Because I am not the thoughts, I can now make more objective decisions about how I respond to those thoughts without being burdened by the weight of their content.

Likewise, during the practice of mindfulness, we invite all experiences – be they pleasurable or not – as plain experiences. We do so without making any judgments, without assigning value, without labelling them good or bad, desirable or undesirable. These attitudes cultivated during mindfulness practices gradually impact the way we live our lives, outside the practice. It is similar to the phenomenon of pumping iron in the gym regularly, resulting in you being able to carry heavier loads at your workplace. One causes the other.

Maybe you are stepping out of your house to go for a walk and the sky slowly turns dark. It is going to be a heavy downpour.

Would that bring frustration and resentment – as the rain will surely spoil your plans for the day?

A mindfulness practitioner would receive the dark clouds with acceptance, and then do what needs to be done, which is to grab an umbrella. She would see that there is nothing intrinsically bad or good about the rain.

It is the rejection of the unfavourable that causes difficult emotions. We expect that the weather will be always good, that things will always go as planned. By letting go of that, we accept the rain as it is and respond with objectivity. In so doing, we gain an acceptance of things beyond our control and a greater compassion for ourselves.

With acceptance, every thought or experience is an unexpected visitor. We do not turn them away, nor do we expect them to stay forever. We let them come and go. Being mindful is like being an ocean that accepts waters from all rivers without rejection.

LIKES AND DISLIKES

Most of the time, we spend our time doing things that we like, while staying away from things that we dislike. We do know, of course, that some of our roles require that we do things that we dislike, like clearing the garbage can, or doing the dishes, or even spending time with our family.

There is also this belief that we should go beyond our likes and dislikes. However, that doesn't work, because doing what I like brings happiness and comfort, while doing the opposite brings unhappiness and discomfort.

But yet we know that we do need to do what ought to be done for a variety of reasons. So what should I prioritise? The sweet drink on the table, which may aggravate my diabetic condition, or the glass of water? I could enjoy that sugary drink, but I might suffer later. The mindfulness solution to this dilemma is: Do not try to grapple with the rationale behind what needs to be done. Instead, we deal with our issues through the attitude of 'non-striving'.

So, rather than 'striving' to deal with our issues head-on, which merely creates greater stress and pressure, we approach them

'IN MINDFULNESS, ACCEPTANCE ALWAYS
COMES FIRST, CHANGE COMES AFTER.'

– SHAMASH ALIDINA

indirectly through mindfulness practices by cultivating an attitude before aiming at an action that may (or may not) solve
the issue.

We all know what is right for us to a large extent. We have
learned all that we need to be well, physically and mentally,
from school and from our upbringing. Through knowledge and
insights from our life experiences, both negative and positive,
we have the opportunity to generate insights into what we
need to do and what we need to avoid to be well and happy.
Yet, what we lack is the mental strength to do what needs to

be done. Mindfulness practices strengthen our minds to do just that.

By bringing the awareness of being into our life, we accept ourselves and our supposed issues as they are. As a result, we are better able to make the right choices that contribute to our wellbeing instead of entertaining the subjectivity of likes and dislikes.

Non-striving is indeed one of the key attitudes of mindfulness. Take the struggle out of handling the issues and focus on the practice. Truly there is no goal as you practise. Just like your breathing, which happens without a conscious goal, you can anchor yourself to the understanding that you are 'doing for the sake of doing' and not for the sake of a cherished goal.

INTRODUCING MINDFUL MOVEMENT

Mindfulness is not all about sitting still but can also be cultivated while you are in motion. The practice of mindful movement is different from routine physical activities. In mindful movement practice, we bring the attitude of attention and acceptance into the practice, noticing the body as it is from moment to moment without wanting to change it. This is a stark contrast to aerobic exercises, modern hatha yoga sessions or fitness classes, where you are placed in the doing mode.

In mindful movement practices, we engage in gentle stretches and movements. We learn not to push the body to unnatural extremes. We are also not interested in achieving a perfect posture.

Instead, we do the stretches to our limit and bring awareness into the practice consistently. While you are at it, you may feel slight discomfort. Instead of judging that sensation, bring awareness to it, and see it as another experience among the many that you have every day. The ability to notice without judgment is what it is all about.

As you continue bringing awareness to your movements, it may become second nature for you to bring this into your movements throughout the day.

PRACTICE 7

MINDFUL MOVEMENT

This practice can be done while sitting or standing. The intention is to pay attention to your movements and bring acceptance to the experiences. As you are performing the steps below, bring your attention to the muscles contracting or stretching while you are in motion. Notice the changes taking place within the body.

1. While seated or standing, gently bring awareness to your body.

2. Do a quick scan of your body from your feet to the top of your head.

3. When ready, raise your left arm slowly and steadily until your fingers are pointed at the ceiling/sky.

4. Gently and slowly lower your arm back to its original position.

5. Do the same with your right arm.

6. Gently lift your left foot off the floor as high as you can.

7. Gently lower your left foot back on to the floor.

8. Do the same with your right foot.

Post-practice inquiry

1. What changes did you notice?

2. Do you have a sequence of movements that you can easily remember?

3. What sensations did you feel in different parts of your body?

4. Did thoughts enter your mind? How did you treat the presence or absence of thoughts?

DAY 8: THE FUTURE IN THE PRESENT MOMENT

The future is very important to all of us. We spend most of our waking time planning for the future so that we can live our lives happily and as we expect it to be. We plan for holidays, staycations, family dinners, hoping that they are going be pleasant and happy events. And as discussed before, all of this planning for the future takes place in the present.

Nobody plans to be unhappy in the present or in the future. So, is there a way of being happy in any given moment, in various situations and events of our lives? The answer is yes, according to happiness scientists. And mindfulness helps us with this by allowing us to shift to a new paradigm. I call this new paradigm, the *happiness paradigm*, inspired by the insights I have gained from my practice of mindfulness and happiness science as we know it today.

HAPPINESS PARADIGM

All of us value our personal wellbeing and happiness. We find it uncomfortable and difficult to be unhappy, distressed, stressed, miserable, depressed or anxious; these experiences feel alien to our being, like a splinter lodged in the finger, waiting to be removed.

In the absence of these difficult emotions, we feel restored to our baseline level of wellbeing. But this baseline state is not the state of wellbeing that we actively seek. To secure wellbeing, we seek emotions such as love, joy, satisfaction, happiness or serenity. After attaining it, we also seek to increase the frequency of these positive emotions in our lives, so that we can maximise the experience of happiness over time. When asked if our day was great, our minds quickly search for experiences in the day that created these positive emotions. Happiness and wellbeing, then, are not the absence of negative emotions alone but the presence of positive emotions.

But we have to acknowledge that both positive and negative emotions are not entirely within our control. They may appear in situations where we expect them, but they may also not appear. For instance, you planned the perfect birthday for your child but everything went wrong. There can be many slips between the cup and the lip.

Therefore, to believe that we need only positive emotions and experiences to be happy is idealistic and unrealistic. To be happy, then, we need a different paradigm. One that is real-istic and possible. Mindfulness practice and evidence tell us that mindfulness practitioners enjoy the psychological skills to:

- Flexibly deploy attention

- Accept

- Generate different perspectives

The skill of *flexibly deploying attention* refers to the ability to voluntarily deploy and direct attention to things and memories. This would mean that in any given situation, mindfulness practitioners can choose to see the positive and focus on what is working. They would be able to acknowledge and be aware of their strengths and values.

The ability to *accept* is the capacity to not be reactive and to stay open to any experience, especially the negative emotions caused by unfavourable situations and events. This allows mindfulness practitioners to expect negative emotions caused by unfavourable outcomes. They stay present by not rejecting or avoiding these difficult emotions and respond with poise and calm, as opposed to going on a downward spiral.

The skill to *generate different perspectives* comes from the insight that thoughts are not facts but perspectives. Though the truth or reality can be one, perspectives can be many. Like the men who look at the same mountain from four directions; each has a different perspective, and yet all of them are right from their perspective. We live in a world where we operate with perspectives more than truths or facts. This is how garage sales and secondhand stores make money – one man's trash is another man's treasure. Mindfulness helps us to shift perspectives by interpreting it with purpose. Discovering our disposition and meaning helps us interpret events, situations and experiences purposefully.

This skill also allows us to be ethical in the way we make decisions in our lives for ourselves and others. The objectivity with which we interpret allows us to stay away from the subjectivity of likes, dislikes and strong emotions that may otherwise sway our judgment in favour of the unwholesome. Ethical considerations are key to the way of being happy and flourishing. What we do and say affects the people around us, as no man is an island. All of us live in an interconnected world where everyone's wellbeing matters.

These three psychological skills allow us to be happy through *attention to the positive, acceptance of the negative* and *purposeful interpretation.* I call this the happiness paradigm.

My practice of mindfulness has helped me be happy most of the time (let's be realistic, not all the time). When my mind reports unfavourable outcomes, it automatically shifts to the positive after accepting the negative and finds ways to see what I can learn from the experience. I must say that this way of *being* happy (not *becoming* happy) is a gradual outcome born of sustained mindfulness practice and not something that you convince yourself with.

YOU ARE NOT THE ROLE

A CEO gets home after a long day at work and tells his wife to bring him a drink. The wife retorts, 'Am I your secretary?' Frustrated, he walks into his teenage daughter's room to see if she has been studying for her exams which are around the corner. He finds her on her smartphone, and scolds her for not focusing on her exam preparations. The daughter gets angry that she is being bossed around like his staff, who are always at his beck and call.

This is a classic illustration of how we bring our roles into spaces where they are not needed. Roles are not absolute, and neither are they forever. We pick a role up, and we can also let them go, if we know how to do that.

The role of a parent is born along with the birth of a child. A name is given with one's birth. A designation is born along with a job and its description. Some roles last longer and some shorter. But the fact remains that the roles do not outlive your nature as a human being. These roles have birth dates and expiry dates as well. The roles depend on you for existence, but you can exist independent of the roles.

Build a list of the various roles that you play on a given day (e.g., parent, child, employer, employee, friend, spouse) and reflect on each of them in terms of three factors:

- How important is that role to you?

- How much time and energy do you invest in that role?

- Are you demanding too much of yourself in that role?

Each of our roles has its limits. By being mindful of their limits, we can effortlessly maximise the effectiveness of each of our roles. For example, when I enter my office, I am a member of staff, and I nurture and play that role. When I step out of the office, I am no longer a member of staff. When I reach home, I should be mindful of being a parent, spouse, son or daughter. I do not bring my role as a CEO home. Or else there will come a time when someone at home is going to give me a rude awakening.

It is perfectly fine to be the boss at your workplace and be bossed around at home. We need to learn to let go of our roles in appropriate situations. This ability naturally develops as we regard our roles as something that we have picked up and are ready to let go of when the need arises.

My mother expresses this role of dissociation very well in her native tongue. When she is ill, she doesn't say, 'I am unwell'; she says, 'The body is unwell'. To me, this is a priceless piece of wisdom – though I took it for granted for many years without appreciating its profundity.

'NO ONE OWNS YOU, I KNOW THAT.
NO ONE OWNS ME. NO ONE OWNS ANYONE.
WE JUST GET TO BORROW EACH
FOR A WHILE.'

– JON COURTENAY GRIMWOOD

This understanding of the self can be extended to other areas of our beliefs. For example, it makes sense to say 'I have a job' as opposed to 'I am the job'. Yet, when it comes to behaviour, we do exactly the opposite. We behave as if we are the job. When we fail in our job, we take it that 'I have failed'. When the job gets outsourced, we feel 'I have no more value'. By being mindful about your choice of words, you can cultivate a healthy attitude in the core of your being. You are not the role. You behold a role.

With mindfulness, I have learned to look at everything I 'own' – including the roles I inhabit – in a healthy way. I have learned to understand that nothing is absolutely owned by me. Instead, I see myself as a trustee of the things I own. Trustees do not own anything except the responsibility invested in them to play their designated roles well and take care of the things entrusted to them. And while I do not own anything absolutely, I enjoy what I have with mindfulness and wisdom. This wisdom does not remove the responsibility I have pertaining to the role but rather makes me aware of the responsibility beyond my likes and dislikes.

FORGIVENESS

Forgiveness is another difficult thing for us human beings. In the past, I found it very hard to forgive people who had wilfully done me harm. But then I asked myself if I had done the same to others, either consciously or unconsciously, and the answer was a definite yes. I wished that those people who had been hurt by my actions and behaviour could forgive me.

And if I was deserving of forgiveness, surely those who had harmed me deserved to be forgiven too. Essentially, I am no different from them as a human being. As I keep reflecting, I realise that forgiveness doesn't mean we are validating the wrongful actions that people have done to us. All we are doing is letting go of the unwholesome feelings that we have harboured since – the bitterness and hurt that arise anew each time we recall the wrongs. It doesn't make sense to let these negative feelings continue to affect our wellbeing long after the incident has passed. We can let go of the pain by forgiving those who have hurt us.

And the time to do that is right now. Take a pause from reading this book and spend the next minute forgiving someone whom you have always wanted to forgive. How does it feel to do this?

'WE MUST DEVELOP AND
MAINTAIN THE CAPACITY TO
FORGIVE. HE WHO IS DEVOID
OF THE POWER TO FORGIVE IS
DEVOID OF THE POWER TO LOVE.
THERE IS SOME GOOD IN THE
WORST OF US AND SOME EVIL
IN THE BEST OF US. WHEN WE
DISCOVER THIS, WE ARE LESS
PRONE TO HATE OUR ENEMIES.'

- MARTIN LUTHER KING

In experiments at the University of North Carolina at Chapel Hill, it was found that practising loving kindness meditation increased positive emotions and decreased negative emotions. I invite you to try out the practice at the end of this chapter.

I AM ALWAYS A WORK-IN-PROGRESS

I take comfort in telling anyone I meet that I am a work-in-progress. I am not a statue that was carved and sculpted to be a perfect masterpiece. I am still being moulded, and forever it shall be so.

I am ready to be remodelled in the hands of the world's greatest sculptor, time. In the present moment, I let myself be crafted by the insights I gain from awareness, attention and acceptance.

I am not perfect, as a perfect being is but a figment of the imagination. Perfection is always a judgment in terms of thoughts, feelings and behaviour. In my essential state of being, there can be no judgments. Awareness can neither judge nor be judged.

All that I am is awareness in any present moment. And so are you. Seeing yourself as a work-in-progress allows you to make mistakes and learn, to fail and keep trying without striving, and finally to accept that you are not a painting on the wall of perfection.

You learn to accept yourself as a being capable of feeling pain but not be susceptible to it. You learn how to fail but not be a failure. To be successful but not be carried away by it. To direct attention flexibly to what has worked and is working well. To accept any experience and respond to it. To be happy by interpreting situations differently when needed. To find purpose in things that may change and perhaps accept purposelessness too.

The only thing you are certain of is that you are awareness and that you are aware of all that is happening to your body-sense-mind complex.

I am a constant work-in-progress. There is no performance

appraisal, there are no KPIs, there are no goals as I cultivate mindfulness in my life. All I know is that I practise mindfulness with sincere intention.

HOW ELSE CAN MINDFULNESS HELP YOU?

Research over the last few decades has shown that mindfulness practices benefit you in many ways. They can:

- **Improve your mental health**
  As your brain learns to respond rather than react to situations, you will find your stress levels reduced, emotions regulated and resilience strengthened. Your emotions and thoughts become healthier, with less dependence on external stimuli for support.

- **Increase your happiness**
  People who meditate are in general happier than people who do not. Mindfulness reminds us that

happiness is now, not in the future, by having the happiness paradigm.

- **Improve relationships**
  Relationships thrive in a space of non-judgment, respect and acceptance. When two people come together with mindfulness, the relationship grows in value, bringing positive emotions and genuine love.

- **Increase positive states of mind**
  When something goes wrong, our minds tend to obsess over what caused it and who to blame. With mindfulness, we can recover from this inherent negative bias in our brain and look at situations more positively.

- **Boost creativity**
  Creativity lies in the executive regions of the brain. And mindfulness works precisely in that region. Now you know the reason why many companies have launched mindfulness programmes for their staff!

- **Improve your attentional and working memory capabilities**

  With the focus on paying attention being a major part of mindfulness practices, you will be able to concentrate on tasks more effectively. The ability to retain what you have learned is also enhanced.

- **Regulate your eating habits**

  In eating mindfully, you become more deliberate and prudent about the choices you make in your diet. Mindfulness also slows down your eating function, allowing the stomach to communicate to the brain that it is full, so that you do not end up over-eating.

- **Reduce depression**

  Mindfulness has been used as complementary therapy alongside medication to help people overcome depression. This happens with acknowledging the mood disorders that are associated with depression. By learning to develop a healthier relationship with them, depression is reduced as a result.

- **Reduce addictive behaviours**

  Addictive behaviours (e.g., smoking, alcohol, drugs, gaming, gambling) have been seen to decrease with mindfulness practices. The mind is able to achieve reduced dependence on these sub-stances and greater resilience to see one through the withdrawal symptoms.

- **Reduce chronic pain**

  Mindfulness saw its earliest successes in people dealing with chronic pain. With eight weeks of mindfulness training, patients were found to have increased ability to respond to pain rather than reacting to it.

- **Enhance resilience**

  Psychological resilience is the ability to adapt and cope in adverse conditions. People in high-stress occupations have found themselves more resilient with mindfulness practices.

- **Reduce stress**

  Research has shown that mindfulness can reduce and prevent stress. This is one of the most immediate and readily recognisable benefits you'll notice from your practices.

- **Reduce anxiety**

  Anxiety is a phenomenon that is rooted in future outcomes. With mindfulness, the mind learns to be in the present, thus reducing the ill effects of anxiety.

As you get motivated by the benefits of mindfulness practices, it is important that you remember that these goals are destinations. While they are good reasons for starting on mindfulness practices, they should not be the pivot of your practice. It is always the present moment that we value as we take the journey to our destination.

PRACTICE 8

LOVING KINDNESS
MEDITATION

As you read the following lines out loud, bring the emotions and feelings that express the same intentions. Pause after saying each line and notice those emotions within you.

May I be well

May I be happy

May I be healthy

May I be free from distress

May all be well

May all be happy

May all be healthy

May all be free from distress

May all attain peace

May all achieve fulfilment

May all see goodness

May none suffer

May all overcome their obstacles

May all attain their cherished desires

May all be happy always

May I be able to pardon all living beings

May they always be able to pardon me

May there be friendship amongst all living beings

May I have no hatred of anyone

WHAT NEXT?

I would like to thank you for completing this eight-day journey with me. I sincerely hope that this experiment with mindfulness has been insightful and rewarding for you. If you discovered just one new thing about yourself during these eight days, you have taken a great step forward.

If you found this book valuable, please do share it with others. Mindfulness gets dusty the moment you shelve the practice – the same as with books.

If you are keen to begin learning mindfulness formally, do consider attending an eight-week mindfulness programme like Mindfulness-Based Wellbeing Enhancement (MBWE).

Different types of eight-week programmes are held all around the world. You will spend two to three hours of your time per week with a mindfulness teacher. These sessions will help you greatly in integrating mindfulness into your life.

You can find out more by doing an internet search for mindfulness programmes in your locality or visit my website (www. centreformindfulness.sg). Do meet the teacher and have a chat about how you would like the workshops to help you. Make sure that you are comfortable with the teacher before embarking on your journey.

Thank you for picking up this book, and for your courage in trying out these experiments. Most of all, may you be well, may you be happy, may you be healthy, may you be free from distress. This is all I wish for you.

BIBLIOGRAPHY

Alidina, Shamash. *The Mindful Way Through Stress.* London: Guilford Press, 2015.

Boyce, Barry (ed.) *The Mindfulness Revolution.* Boston: Shambhala, 2011.

Coleman, Daniel, and Richard J. Davidson. *Altered Traits: Science Reveals How Meditation Changes Your Mind, Brain, and Body.* New York: Avery, 2018.

Kabat-Zinn, Jon. *Full Catastrophe Living.* New York: Bantam Books, 2013.

Kathirasan K, and Sunita Rai. *Mindfulness for the Family: A Parent-Child Workbook for Greater Awareness and Stronger Relationships*. Singapore: Marshall Cavendish Editions, 2021.

Kathirasan K, and Sunita Rai. *Introducing Mindfulness-Based Wellbeing Enhancement: Cultural Adaptation and an 8-Week Path to Wellbeing and Happiness*. London: Routledge, 2023.

Seligman, Martin. *Flourish*. New York: Free Press, 2011.

Siegel, Ronald. *The Mindfulness Solution*. London: Guilford Press, 2010.

ABOUT
THE AUTHOR

Kathirasan K is the Founder CEO of the Centre for Mindfulness (Singapore), which operates in several countries in Asia and delivers mindfulness programmes across the globe to corporations, schools and the public. He is a certified mindfulness teacher (CMT-P) with the International Mindfulness Teachers Association and a mindfulness teacher supervisor. He also has a background in organisational development, leadership and education. He has over two decades of experience in teaching contemplative practices, as well as in training teachers in meditation and philosophy. Kathirasan holds an MBA and a PhD in meditation.